CW00525932

THE STOCKTON & DARLINGTON RAILWAY 175 YEARS

CHARLIE EMETT

SUTTON PUBLISHING

First published in the United Kingdom in 2000 by
Sutton Publishing Limited · Phoenix Mill
Thrupp · Stroud · Gloucestershire · GL5 2BU

British Library Cataloguing in Publication Data
A catalogue record for this book is available from the British Library.

ISBN 0-7509-2511-6

Title page photograph: *Locomotion No. 1* passing a coach on the day the Stockton & Darlington Railway was opened, 1825.

The Northern Echo

Typeset in 11/14pt Photina.
Typesetting and origination by
Sutton Publishing Limited.
Printed and bound in England by
J.H. Haynes & Co. Ltd, Sparkford.

Contents

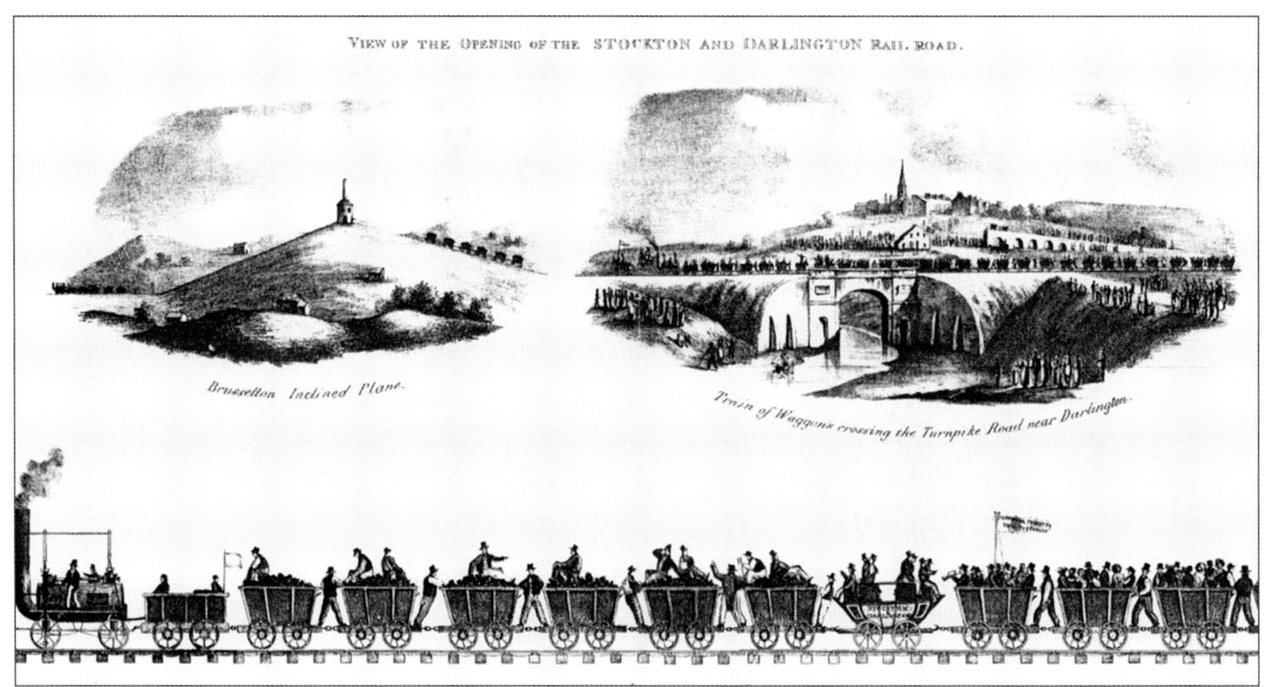

Drawing commemorating the opening of the Stockton & Darlington Railway, 1825.

Acknowledgements and Picture Credits

Exploring the *Northern Echo* picture library is a most enjoyable occupation and my very special thanks go to David Kelly, managing director of the *Northern Echo*, and to Peter Barron, editor of this great newspaper, for allowing me this privilege. Thanks, also, to Peter Chapman and two other guardians of the *Echo* archives, Jane Whitfield and Christine Watson, delightful, intelligent ladies whose ability to make good coffee is only exceeded by their loveliness. To both the Worshipful the Mayor of Darlington, Councillor Dorothy Long, and the Worshipful the Mayor of Stockton-on-Tees, Councillor Pete Andrew, your interest and support are much appreciated. Many thanks. The cover picture of *Locomotion No. 1* is reproduced by kind permission of John Wigston and the Northumbria Tourist Board, and GNER Intercity 225 by Fastline Photographic of York; and I thank you both. To Darlington Railway Centre and Museum, the Ken Hoole Study Centre and, in particular, to Ann Wilson for her help generously given, my thanks, which are also extended to Alistair Downie and Alan Pearce of the excellent Timothy Hackworth Museum, Shildon. Thank you, Richard Barber, for sharing your encyclopedic knowledge of the British railway system with me. Thanks, also, to Ian Storey, locomotive owner, for dealing with my queries so efficiently. Darlington Public Library always turns up trumps, with no query of mine being too much trouble. Thank you, dear ladies. You are a lovely lot! For the typing, my sincere thanks to Eagle Graphics. It is always a real pleasure working with Sutton Publishing's brilliant team: Simon Fletcher, Michelle Tilling, Anne Bennett, Alison Flowers, Joyce Percival and PR specialist Rebecca Nicholls. The secret is that we are all friends pulling in the same direction; and it shows. It is a good feeling. If there are any errors would you return them to me please? They are mine. If I have overlooked anyone I have done so inadvertently and I apologise for this.

Foreword

by THE MAYOR OF STOCKTON

In 1825, the Stockton & Darlington Railway was opened. Passengers travelled from Stockton and thus the advent of travelling by rail started a huge worldwide activity. Unlike earlier schemes, it was the first act by Parliament to enable the carrying of passengers and freight together and the first to use steam locomotion, the new technology.

Fifteen years earlier, the Recorder of Stockton, Leonard Raisbeck, foresaw the impact a railway would have on the economy of the Tees Valley. Few who heard him could have anticipated the profound influence his visionary statement was to have across the globe. On 10 October 1825, the regular passenger service commenced. Stockton was blessed at that time with a number of eminent persons, all with great foresight and imagination. Together, they proposed further developments that had the effect of establishing rail transport over a widening area, but Stockton will remain, for ever, the site where the first regular passenger service by steam locomotive started.

I wish to thank Mr Emett for his exhaustive research and preparation of this book. It is a significant addition to aid others to understand the role that Stockton has played in the development of rail transport and the 175th anniversary of the first run is an important milestone to recall.

Councillor Pete Andrew
The Worshipful the Mayor of The Borough of Stockton-on-Tees, 2000–1

Foreword

by THE MAYOR OF DARLINGTON

The 175th anniversary of the opening of the Stockton & Darlington Railway and the beginning of a new millennium is an appropriate time to reflect on our past and to look forward to our future. In conjunction with this propitious occasion, Darlington author Charlie Emett tells the story, in words and pictures, of how this famous railway line developed and of how, largely because of it, a railway system became established throughout the world. Darlington was always at the forefront of railway development and has continued to be the centre of expertise in locomotive and other forms of engineering to the present day. I am delighted, as Mayor of Darlington, to be associated with this book and the momentous events it celebrates.

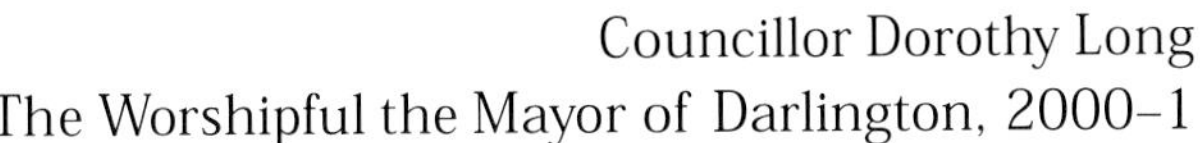

Councillor Dorothy Long
The Worshipful the Mayor of Darlington, 2000–1

Introduction

The Stockton & Darlington Railway, the first public railway worked by steam, marked the real beginning of the railway age, that great symbol of Victorian enterprise and prosperity. The railway's opening on 27 September 1825 set the pattern for the development of railway systems throughout the world; and its use of locomotives for public freight traffic was awe-inspiring.

From earliest times until the sixteenth century people travelled mostly on foot or on horseback. Coal from inland collieries was carried in sacks slung across the backs of packhorses, mules and asses along roads that were impassable by carts. As public highways gradually improved, horse-drawn vehicles came into more general use. At first, a cart pulled by a horse conveyed roughly 1 ton a day for about 10 miles, the load later being increased to 2 tons per cart on aiding gradients.

For hundreds of years planks were used to facilitate movement across soft or uneven sections of highway; and towards the end of the eighteenth century iron straps were fitted to the planks to reduce wear. Simultaneously, some wagons were fitted with flanged wheels to keep them on the road, while, for the same reason, horizontal timber tracks were fitted with cast-iron plates with an upstanding lip. These timber rails, called wagonways, plateways and tramways, were all more or less synonymous and came to be known as railways.

Thomas Newcomen (1663–1729) devised a 'fire machine' to pump water from the tin mines of his native Cornwall. In 1712, after years of experiment, he built his 'atmospheric engine', the first practical and reliable steam engine which, though low in efficiency, served its purpose and was used throughout Europe to pump water out of mines. It had an externally heated boiler and a vertical cylinder.

Scottish engineer James Watt (1738–1819), the principal inventor of the steam engine, made great improvements to this design. In 1763 he added a condenser, and in 1781 he introduced the conversion of the to-and-fro motion to rotary motion and, later, double action whereby steam was introduced first to one side of the piston, then the other, which doubled the power. In 1784 Watt patented an application of his engine for the movement of carriages, but nothing came of this at that time. Also in this year the Scottish engineer William Symington (1763–1831) applied steam locomotives to navigation and the following year, 1785, fitted a 12-horsepower engine to a boat drawing barges along the Forth and Clyde canal.

Richard Trevithick (1771–1833) invented the high-pressure steam engine, which he patented in 1802 and used on the Pen-y-Darren tramway at Merthyr Tydfil, where it hauled 25 tons. Unlike Newcomen's and Watt's engines, which worked on a low pressure of less than 1 atmosphere, Trevithick's engines were high pressure of about 50lb per square in, 3½ atmospheres, which meant they could be lighter and smaller but achieve the same power output. He continued to develop his ideas, making the boiler the frame for the engine itself, so that the whole lot could be moved from place to place with ease.

In 1811 John Blenkinsop (1783–1831) patented a locomotive engine worked by a rack or toothed rail, which was used at Middleton Colliery, near Leeds. The following year William Chapman (1749–1832) built an engine worked by an endless chain that was used on the Heaton Colliery Railway in 1813.

That same year the manager of the Wylam Colliery Railway, William Hedley (1779–1843), used his engine, *Puffing Billy*, for the first time on that railway. The owner of the colliery, Captain Christopher Blackett, built the railway there with wooden rails which were not strong enough to sustain the weight of an engine. In 1808 he replaced them with cast-iron plate rails, always seeking a means of transport that was cheaper and quicker than horses. William Hedley initially made an engine mounted on a carriage, but it tended to be short of steam and was not a success. He built two more, both to his own design, *Puffing Billy*, in 1813, and *Wylam Dilly*, in 1814. Both were well designed but their weight was concentrated on four wheels and they were too heavy for the plate rails. He had them remounted on eight wheels to spread the load and they worked satisfactorily. When the plate rails were replaced by wedge rails, Hedley rebuilt his locomotive to his original four-wheel design and gave the wheels flanges. This was successful and the locomotive worked well. *Wylam Dilly* was converted into a paddleboat engine in 1822 when, mounted on a keel, *Tom and Jerry*, it hauled four more keels loaded with coal.

On 9 June 1781 the most famous of all those involved with the development of the railways, George Stephenson (1781–1848), was born in a cottage alongside Captain Blackett's Wylam Colliery Railway. He was the son of a mechanic who operated a Newcomen atmospheric steam engine. At an early age, and without a formal education, Stephenson went to work and began operating a Newcomen engine. He also enrolled at night school to learn to read and write. In 1812 his genius with the steam engine won him the post of engine-wright (chief mechanic) at Killingworth Colliery, where he was in charge of all the machinery of the 'Grand Allies', a coalition of coal-owning families. He was fortunate enough to have a company horse with the job.

His first wife died leaving him with a young son, Robert, who was sent to Newcastle to study mathematics. Every night father and son worked on Robert's homework together.

In 1813 George Stephenson visited a neighbouring colliery to examine a steam boiler on wheels, built by John Blenkinsop to haul coal out of the mines. It broke down frequently and George thought that he could improve on the design. In 1814, after consulting Lord Ravensworth, the principal owner of Killingworth, he built an engine, the *Blucher*, that could draw eight loaded wagons carrying 30 tons of coal at 4mph. Not satisfied, George sought to modify this further and introduced the 'steam blast' by which exhaust steam was redirected up the chimney, pulling air after it and increasing the draught. This new design made the locomotive a real practicality; the *Blucher* was the first of several locomotives George built for Killingworth and other collieries. In addition, at the same time as Humphrey Davy invented his miner's safety lamp, George Stephenson also invented a similar device, known as the 'Geordie', for which he received a public testimonial of £1,000.

When George Stephenson was appointed engine-wright at Killingworth Colliery, the only railway used at the colliery was constructed of cast iron, a yard long and with square joints.

It could only bear the weight of a chaldron loaded with 53cwt of coal or a gross weight of 4 tons. In order to prevent the shock to the wheels from the square joints, George, in conjunction with William Losh of the Walker Ironworks, patented a rail with half a lap joint or with one half of the end of the rails cut away longitudinally for about 2 in. Thus, when the ends of two rails were laid together, they had the same breadth of top at each joint as the solid part of the track, which eliminated the shock to the carriage passing over it.

George Stephenson also made improvements to the construction of railway chairs and wheels. Moreover, through his work at Killingworth Colliery, where he was constantly building and improving the design of his locomotives, he quickly gained a national reputation that attracted curiosity and attention throughout Europe.

During the eighteenth century coal from the deep, seaward dipping mines of the Tyne hinterland was easily transported along short wagonways to the navigable Tyne and Wear rivers. Coal from the South Durham coalfield around Bishop Auckland, on the other hand, was easier to mine, but output, which should have been in millions of tons per annum, was limited to only thousands of tons because the coal was usually conveyed on packhorses, mules and asses, an expensive and inefficient means of transport.

There were two practical alternatives to road transport for the conveyance of minerals, goods and passengers – canals and railways. In 1768 James Brindley and Whitworth, his assistant, surveyed a canal, as did Ralph Todd, also in 1768. Both projects had to be abandoned because of the finance required, which was not forthcoming.

Several Stockton entrepreneurs wished to break the monopoly the colliery owners had on the movement of coal, and saw the building of a canal or a railway to serve the South Durham coalfield as a means of achieving this. It was, after all, the beginning of the nineteenth century and Stockton was already an important commercial centre served by a busy, prosperous port with a long-established trade in farm produce and lead.

By the late 1780s many of Britain's early canals had been built and the country was caught up in canal mania – a new wave of canal building that peaked in about 1792. Between 1791 and 1795 some forty-eight new canals were authorised with a capital of £7 million. Then, in 1793, Britain went to war with France and this caused inflation. As a result, canal construction cost more and took longer to complete. The future was fraught with difficulties and uncertainty.

On 18 September 1810 a celebratory dinner was held in Stockton's Town House, the Town Hall, to mark the opening of the 'cut', which was designed to shorten the channel of the River Tees between Stockton and Portrack by removing an awkward bend. At this event Leonard Raisbeck, Stockton's Recorder, moved a resolution that a committee be appointed to enquire into the feasibility of building a railway or a canal from Stockton to Winston via Darlington for the carriage of mineral and other traffic from North Yorkshire and South Durham.

In 1811 the appointed committee agreed that either a canal or a railway would be of great advantage to the locality and proposed to report thereon to 'a meeting of gentlemen, merchants and others who were desirous of the undertaking'.

On Friday 17 January 1812, at a meeting held at the King's Head, Darlington, it was resolved to employ the eminent engineer Rennie to survey the proposed route and to explore the options, which he did in 1813.

For six years public opinion was divided as to whether a canal or railway would best further the interests of commerce and benefit the proprietors; and the canal had the advantage. For many years steam navigation had been capable of 7mph, whereas no locomotive could travel faster than 4 or 5mph. Nor were there any generally accepted proposals for the railway to supersede the stage-coach. It was designed almost exclusively for carrying goods in a better and more expeditious way. For various reasons no progress was made one way or the other. On 31 July 1818, at a public meeting held in Stockton with the Earl of Strathmore presiding, Leonard Raisbeck, the principal speaker, recommended that the canal should commence at the north end of Stockton and go via Darlington to Winston Bridge, following the route first set by Whitworth in 1768 and again by Rennie in 1813.

The estimated cost of the main canal from the Tees at Stockton to Darlington, its continuation to Winston Bridge and branch canals to Yarm, Croft Bridge and Piercebridge came to a total of £205,283, double that of the suggested cost of the proposed railway. The estimated revenue from all sources was £57,850 per annum.

The nature of the land the canal would have to cross was unfavourable, with fifty locks required in under 30 miles. It was an area of thinly scattered farmhouses, no factories and little commerce. Half a century later South Durham would be transformed by thriving coal mines and much new industry, but in 1818 the landscape was rural. So the grand plans for the Stockton to Winston Bridge Canal came to nothing.

There were two rival groups of promoters: those advocating a canal and those for a railway. On 4 September 1818, at a meeting in Darlington, a committee was appointed to consider the relative merits of the two schemes. On Friday 13 November 1818 'a highly respectable meeting was held in the Town Hall, Darlington, for the purpose of taking into consideration the committee's report on the survey taken a few years ago by Mr Rennie for a canal and, more lately, by Mr Overton for a railway between Stockton and the collieries in the Auckland district by way of Darlington'. Dr John Ralph Fenwick presided and the reports of Mr Rennie on the canal scheme and of Mr Overton in favour of the railway project were read separately. Also presented was the report on the relative merits of the two schemes. The principal speakers were Jonathan Backhouse, Edward Pease, John Grimshaw and William Stobart Junior, each of whom strongly recommended the adoption of a railway in preference to a canal.

In a fact-filled speech, Jonathan Backhouse ridiculed the exaggerated claims of those promoting the canal scheme and demolished their arguments. He summed up by maintaining that the railway scheme 'on whatever side we see it, whether as a public benefit or as a private adventure, it powerfully urges the undertaking and affords a rational and well grounded expectation of an ample reward to the subscribers'. Edward Pease heartily endorsed Jonathan Backhouse's conclusions and the meeting was in harmony with him. The only prospectus ever issued of the Stockton & Darlington Railway company was drawn up at that meeting. Edward Pease (1767–1858) was a Quaker and from a family of prominent Darlington Quakers. He was a highly respected woollen merchant and banker, and he passionately believed in the idea of a Stockton & Darlington Railway. It was he who persuaded fellow Quakers the Gurneys in Norwich and Richardson's banking firm in London to provide badly needed investment capital and additional loans to ensure that the railway became a reality. So deep was Quaker investment that as progress was made the Stockton & Darlington Railway was frequently nicknamed the 'Quaker Line'.

In 1818, the year the promotors employed the railway engineer George Overton to survey the original line, there was still a good deal of uncertainty about the route the railway should take. It was resolved therefore to call in a consultant, Robert Stevenson, a lighthouse engineer from Edinburgh, to report on the proposed line.

Stevenson recommended the setting up of a management committee, and this was done. Helped wholeheartedly by George Overton, this committee set about its work vigorously. A voluminous correspondence began with landowners along the route of the proposed line, some of whom were strongly opposed to the project. One of the fiercest opponents was Lord Darlington of Raby Castle whose attitude was implacable. When Francis Milburn, solicitor to the promotion, questioned George Overton regarding the calculated cost of the line, Overton 'undertook to make the railway a single road at £2,000 a mile: formed for double at £2,400 a mile: if double, £2,800 a mile'.

The first bill for the Stockton & Darlington Railway faced formidable opposition, but its supporters were determined. One MP with considerable parliamentary influence, Mr T. Grey of Millfield Hill, wrote to Joseph Pease Junior on 22 February 1819 informing him of the lobbying he had done in support of the project; but 'not to Lord Tankerville because he is almost superannuated and never goes to the House'. The bill failed at the second reading, but only just: 106 votes against, 93 in favour. It was rejected by a majority of only 13 and this was attributed to the very short space of time allowed for completing the survey and making friendly arrangements with the landowners.

With the defeat of the first bill, the promotors determined to have another survey made with a view to adopting a different route. The committee resolved 'that no time should be lost in endeavouring to conciliate all those whose interest or opinions are opposed to the measure'.

The first route chosen on Overton's recommendation and survey was from Stockton via Darlington, Summerhouse, Ingleton and Hilton to the West Auckland coalfields, cutting through one of the Duke of Cleveland's fox coverts, which was naturally of greater consequence to the nobility than the promoters of a public railway.

Overton undertook another survey, which was completed by 1 September 1820. On 29 September he submitted a report to the committee who, in a manifesto dated November 1820, endorsed Overton's observations. The manifesto shows that 'the expense of constructing a railway road on the intended line is estimated at £82,000 the greater part of which is subscribed'.

An application was made for another act early in 1820, but it was delayed because of the death of King George III. On 12 February 1820, at a meeting of the committee held in Yarm and presided over by Thomas Meynell, a letter from the company's parliamentary agents was read out advising that the application be deferred until the 1820–1 session of Parliament, which it was. The Stockton & Darlington Railway Company fought as hard for the second bill as for the first, attempting to influence as many supporters as possible. Their efforts met with success and the second bill received royal assent in April 1821. The chief promoter, the man who more than anyone else promoted the passing of the act authorising the construction of the Stockton & Darlington Railway, was Edward Pease.

At this time George Stephenson was laying the 8-mile-long Hetton Colliery Railway across very undulating terrain. This was the first railway to be operated independently of animal power and was completed in 1822. The many improvements and modifications to the permanent way and the rolling stock Stephenson had patented brought him to the attention of Edward Pease. Some time earlier, in about 1812, George Stephenson had been asked to survey a line from the collieries in the Auckland area to Darlington and Stockton, so the two men would most certainly have known each other.

George Stephenson learned of a plan to build a railway employing drafthorses from Stockton to Darlington to facilitate the exploitation of a rich vein of coal, and was interested in this and wrote to Edward Pease in Darlington requesting an interview regarding the proposed line. A meeting was arranged for 19 April 1821 and George, his son Robert and Nicholas Wood left Killingworth for Newcastle on horseback, travelled from there to 32 miles-distant Stockton by coach, then walked the 12 miles from Stockton to Darlington along the proposed line of the railway. Following the interview with Edward Pease, the three of them walked the 18 miles to Durham. Within 3 miles of their destination, the Travellers' Rest, Nicholas Wood collapsed with exhaustion, but had to continue because their beds had been booked. George Stephenson teased Wood about this incident until just before his own death.

The meeting resulted in George Stephenson being employed by the Stockton & Darlington Railway. He began surveying the new line in the autumn of 1821, assisted by John Dixon, whose grandfather George Dixon of Cockfield had been involved in surveying and promoting the canal scheme of 1767. Robert Stephenson left his job as a pit viewer and joined the surveying party.

Edward Pease, unhappy with the original route surveyed by George Overton, was delighted at the alterations made to it by George Stephenson which made the line 3 miles shorter than Overton's. It ran close to Darlington and, at a total cost of £64,640, was also much cheaper to build. When the survey was complete, Robert Stephenson's name was shown on the plans as the engineer; but it was his father who was responsible to the company. The survey was so well received that, on 22 January 1822, George Stephenson was appointed engineer to the company 'at a salary of £600 per annum, the said salary being understood to cover all the services and expenses of himself and assistant surveyors'.

It is significant that the Stockton & Darlington Railway Company's first act contained no powers for the use of locomotives, whereas in the company's second act they are empowered to 'make, erect and set up one permanent or fixed steam engine or other proper machines in such convenient situation' as they chose.

On 23 May 1822, to the peal of church bells, Thomas Meynell of Yarm, as Chairman of the company, accompanied by the Mayor, the Recorder and members of Stockton Corporation, cut the first sod and laid the first rail at St John's Well, Stockton, at what is now Bridge Road. Thomas Meynell may have thought he had cut the first sod, but he did not. One fine evening in the autumn of 1821, while busily engaged on the line's survey and finding himself surrounded by some of the workmen, George Stephenson said, 'Come, give me a spade. Let it never be said that we have not made a beginning.'

There and then, close to St John's Well, he began work on the new railway.

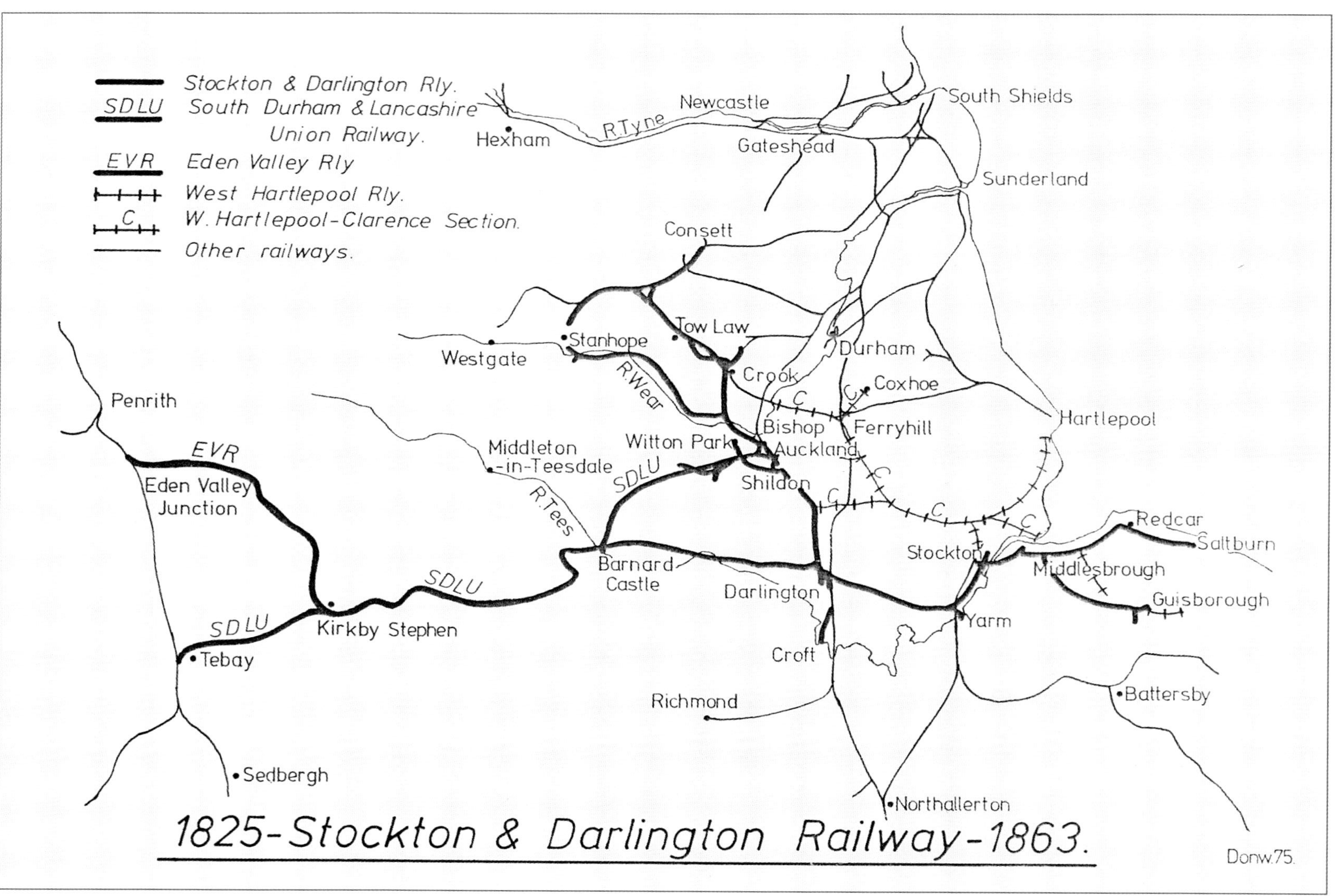

Railways operating in the Stockton and Darlington area between 1825 and 1863.

CHAPTER ONE

How It All Began

An early locomotive engine at Wylam Colliery, which was situated in the Tyneside region where the first railroad was invented. Parallel lines of rails on which wagons run were in vogue about 350 years ago between collieries in Northumberland and the staiths on the River Tyne. At first they were made of wood. Beams of timber 5 or 6 in wide were laid down and fastened to traverse sleepers with pins. The sleepers were then covered with soil to protect the horses' hooves. The first iron railway was constructed in Whitehaven in 1738, but it was not a success. In 1754 wheels were first made of cast iron and the flanged wheel, introduced by Jessop of Loughborough, was generally accepted.

In 1776 John Carr laid down a cast-iron tramway with an upright flange 3 in high and a level surface about 4 in broad at the Duke of Norfolk's colliery near Sheffield. His workmen, whom he meant to benefit but who feared for their livelihood, became violent, tore up the railway and burnt a coal staith. Carr hid in a wood for three days to escape rough treatment at the hands of these miners. In 1791 the wooden rails were rounded at the top and the wheels were hollowed to meet them.

In 1801 the first public railway act was passed by Parliament and the Surrey Iron Railway Company became the first railway company in the world; unfortunately, financially it was a failure. Therefore, the S&DR was not the first public railway, nor even the first railway over which a locomotive engine had passed, but it was the first public railway on which locomotives did the haulage and it was the true beginning of our present railway system.

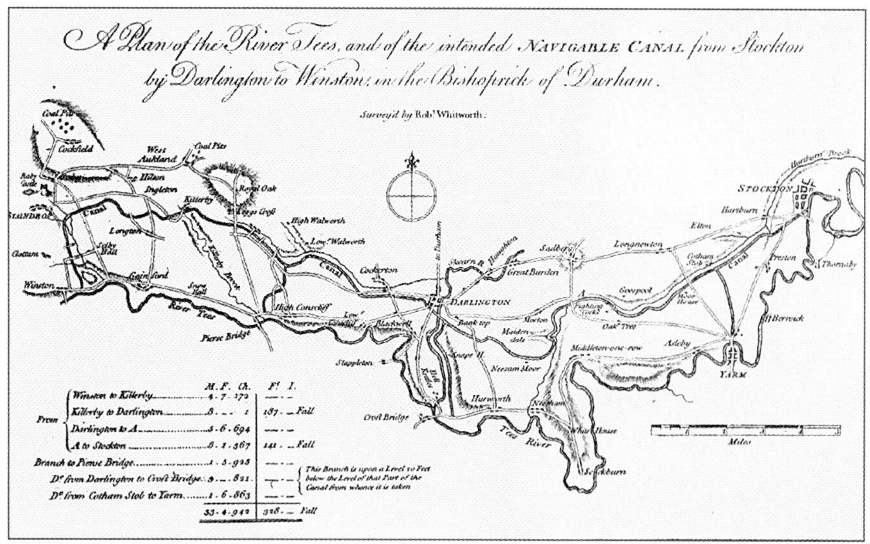

By 1810 parliamentary powers had been obtained for 58 miles of railway in England, 40 miles in Wales and 10 miles in Scotland. All were made for carrying minerals. The conveyance of passengers had not been thought of by the promoters of railway schemes. At this time there were 2,000 miles of canals in England alone, constructed at a cost of £50,000. Many shares were at a premium and some of the canals were paying large dividends. The case for railways looked bad. Only 100 miles of railways were authorised with less than 70 miles in operation, all confined to South Wales. It was estimated at that time that a railway would cost £5,000 per mile, while a canal would cost only £2,000 per mile. But railway promoters argued, with some accuracy, that the advantage of the railway was that it could go to the pit mouth. At a meeting in Darlington in 1812 it was decided to call in Mr Rennie to make a survey as to the best method of communication between Stockton and Winston, which he did. After some time Rennie advised the building of a canal. His calculation showed that previous estimates, based on Robert Whitworth's survey of 1768, were incorrect. The plan of the survey carried out by Whitworth is seen here. In 1818, at a public meeting in Stockton, Leonard Raisbeck recommended that a canal should be built.

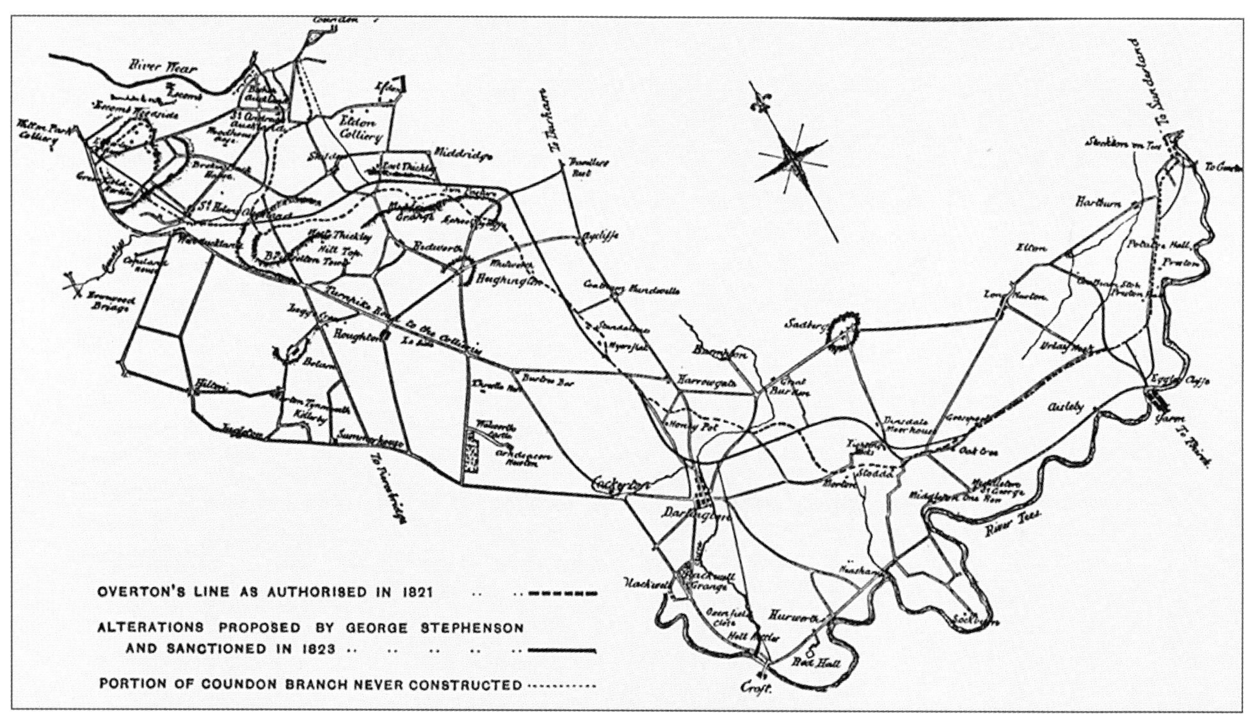

On Friday 13 November 1818, at a meeting in Darlington Town Hall, the relative merits of Mr Rennie's survey of 1813 for a canal and Mr Overton's more recent survey for a railway were discussed. Jonathan Backhouse demolished the arguments for a canal and Edward Pease endorsed him. Between 1813 and 1818 Edward Pease had become convinced of two things: first that an iron railway, not a canal, should be built: secondly, that it should commence at the collieries and terminate at Stockton, taking in Darlington *en route*. The railway won the day. This plan of the S&DR shows Overton's line and George Stephenson's alterations to it.

AT A

MEETING

OF

GENTLEMEN, MERCHANTS, AND OTHERS, FOR THE PURPOSE OF PROMOTING A

Canal or Railway

FROM STOCKTON, BY DARLINGTON,

Westwards,

HELD AT THE

HOUSE OF MR. SCOTT, THE KING's HEAD, IN DARLINGTON, IN THE COUNTY OF DURHAM,

On Friday, the 17th day of January, 1812,

Pursuant to advertisement,—

(The Resolutions of the general Meeting, held on the 18th day of September, 1810, having been read, and the Report of the Committee then appointed having been received and taken into Consideration)—

RESOLVED,

THAT a Survey of the Country or District, through which the proposed Canal or Railway is intended to pass, be forthwith made by Mr. RENNIE. That he be instructed to make a Report as to the practicability of those several measures, their comparative advantages, and the best line or course and extent for each; with an estimate of the expence which will attend the carrying it into effect.

That a Subscription be entered into, in order to defray the expence of such survey, and any other reasonable charges which have already been, or shall hereafter be, incurred relative to the projected undertakings; and that the Committee shall have power to call for such proportion thereof as they shall find necessary, and to direct to whom the same shall be paid.

Minutes of the 1812 meeting convened to discuss the best form of transportation between Stockton and Darlington. At the meeting it was resolved to employ Mr Rennie, the eminent engineer, to make a survey of the ground to discover whether a canal or a railway would best serve the interests of commerce in the area and the proprietors.

4° GEORGII IV. *Cap.* xxxiii. 665

thereof and Persons interested therein respectively (other than and except those specified in the Schedule annexed to this Act).

Power for the Company to erect Steam Engines, and to purchase Land, not exceeding Two Acres in the whole, for that Purpose.

VII. And whereas it will be expedient and necessary for the said Company of Proprietors to erect Steam Engines or other proper Machines in certain Places upon or near to the said Railways or Tramroads by the said recited Act and this Act directed or authorized to be made, for the Purpose of facilitating the Transport, Conveyance, and Carriage of Goods, Merchandize, and other Articles and Things upon and along the same; be it therefore further enacted, That it shall and may be lawful for the said Company of Proprietors, and they are hereby authorized and empowered, from and after the passing of this Act, by themselves or by their Deputies, Agents, Officers, Workmen, or Servants, to make, erect, and set up one permanent or fixed Steam Engine or other proper Machine, in such convenient Situation at or near each of the inclined Planes, which shall be made by virtue or in pursuance of the said recited Act or of this Act, as the said Company of Proprietors shall think proper, and to take and purchase from any Person or Persons, Bodies Politic, Corporate, or Collegiate, or Corporation Aggregate or Sole, who shall be willing to sell the same, any Lands, Tenements, or Hereditaments which may be necessary or convenient for that Purpose, so as the entire Quantity of the Lands, Tenements, or Hereditaments to be taken and appropriated for the Purpose aforesaid do not exceed in the whole Two Acres for any one Engine; and also, with the Consent of the Owner or Owners of the Lands in or through which the same shall be made, to make such and so many Wells, Watercourses, Drains, and other Works for supplying the said Steam Engines and other Machines with Water, as shall be deemed requisite or convenient, and for the Purposes aforesaid, or any of them, to purchase, take, and use the Lands and Grounds of any Person or Persons, Bodies Politic or Collegiate, who shall be willing to sell the same.

Power to make and use locomotive or moveable Engines on the Railway.

VIII. And be it further enacted, That it shall and may be lawful to and for the said Company of Proprietors, or any Person or Persons authorized or permitted by them, from and after the passing of this Act, to make and erect such and so many loco-motive or moveable Engines as the said Company of Proprietors shall from Time to Time think proper and expedient, and to use and employ the same in or upon the said Railways or Tramroads, or any of them, by the said recited Act and this Act directed or authorized to be made, for the Purpose of facilitating the Transport, Conveyance, and Carriage of Goods, Merchandize, and other Articles and Things upon and along the same Roads, and for the Conveyance of Passengers upon and along the same Roads.

Repealing the Part of the recited Act which relates to the Quantity of Land to be purchased for Wharfs.

IX. And whereas it is in and by the said recited Act enacted, that the said Company of Proprietors shall have full Liberty and Power to purchase any Parcel of Land, not exceeding Five Acres in the whole, for the Purpose of making a Wharf or Wharfs: And whereas it may tend to the public Advantage and Accommodation if the said Company of Proprietors be empowered to purchase a greater Quantity of Land than Five Acres, and also to purchase any Messuages or other Buildings for the Purpose of making and erecting a Wharf or Wharfs; and also for the

[*Local.*] 8 *F* Purpose

The first bill applied for by the promoters of the S&DR failed on the second reading. The first bill made no mention of the use of steam engines on the proposed line but the second did, as this extract shows. Application was made for another act early in 1820, but it was delayed because of the death of King George III, finally being passed on 19 April 1821.

On 19 April 1821, the very day the act received royal assent, Edward Pease, one of the principal promoters, received a visit from George Stephenson, who, by 1821, had built up a reputation in the north of England as an experienced engineer. The meeting was fruitful and the following day Pease wrote to Stephenson asking him to survey the proposed route of the S&DR. This letter, dated 28 April 1821, from Killingworth Colliery, is Stephenson's reply. In it he expresses his pleasure that the line can now be built, explains that he cannot help the S&DR committee full time but that he is willing to carry out a survey of the proposed route, to assist the committee with plans and estimates, the allocation of work to various contractors and the supervision of the line's construction.

Killingworth Colliery
April 28th. 1821.

Edwd. Pease Esqr

Sir. I have been favored with your Letter of the 20 Inst & am glad to learn that the Bill has passed for the Darlington Rail Way.
I am much obliged by the favorable sentiments you express towards me: & shall be happy if I can be of service in carrying into execution your Plans.
From the nature of my engagements here and in the neighbourhood, I could not devote the whole of my time to your Rail Way, but I am willing to undertake to survey & mark out the best line of Way within the limits prescribed by the Act of Parliament and also, to assist the Committee with plans & estimates, and in letting to the different Contractors such Work as they might judge it adviseable to do by Contract and also to superintend the execution of the Work–
And I am induced to recommend the whole being

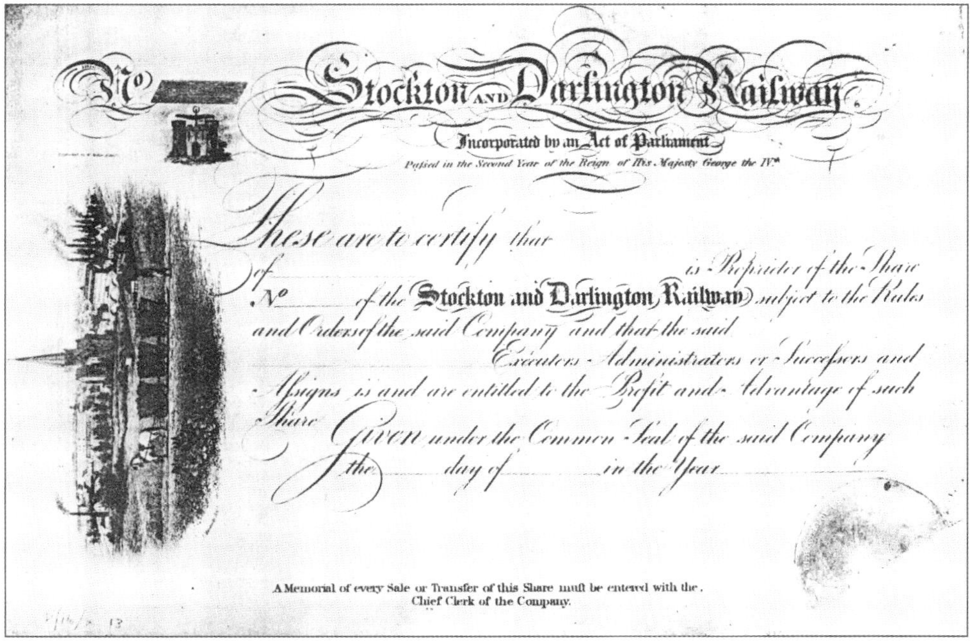

No

Stockton and Darlington Railway.

Incorporated by an Act of Parliament

Passed in the Second Year of the Reign of His Majesty George the IVth

These are to certify that
of is Proprietor of the Share
No of the Stockton and Darlington Railway subject to the Rules
and Orders of the said Company and that the said
Executors Administrators or Successors and
Assigns is and are entitled to the Profit and Advantage of such
Share Given under the Common Seal of the said Company
the day of in the Year

A Memorial of every Sale or Transfer of this Share must be entered with the Chief Clerk of the Company.

It was doubtful whether this share in the Stockton & Darlington Railway, issued in 1822, would be needed because the whole scheme was in jeopardy at this time. Although money had been subscribed by the Peases, the Backhouses and some hundred others, in 1821, £10,000 still needed to be raised. Mr Mewburn, the Company solicitor, was sent to London to enrol new shareholders, but his visit was a failure. He wrote to Edward Pease telling him that the situation was critical because only a few days remained to obtain the necessary money. Mr Pease wrote back to Mr Mewburn stating that as he could not raise an additional farthing in Darlington and its neighbourhood, he would subscribe £10,000 himself.

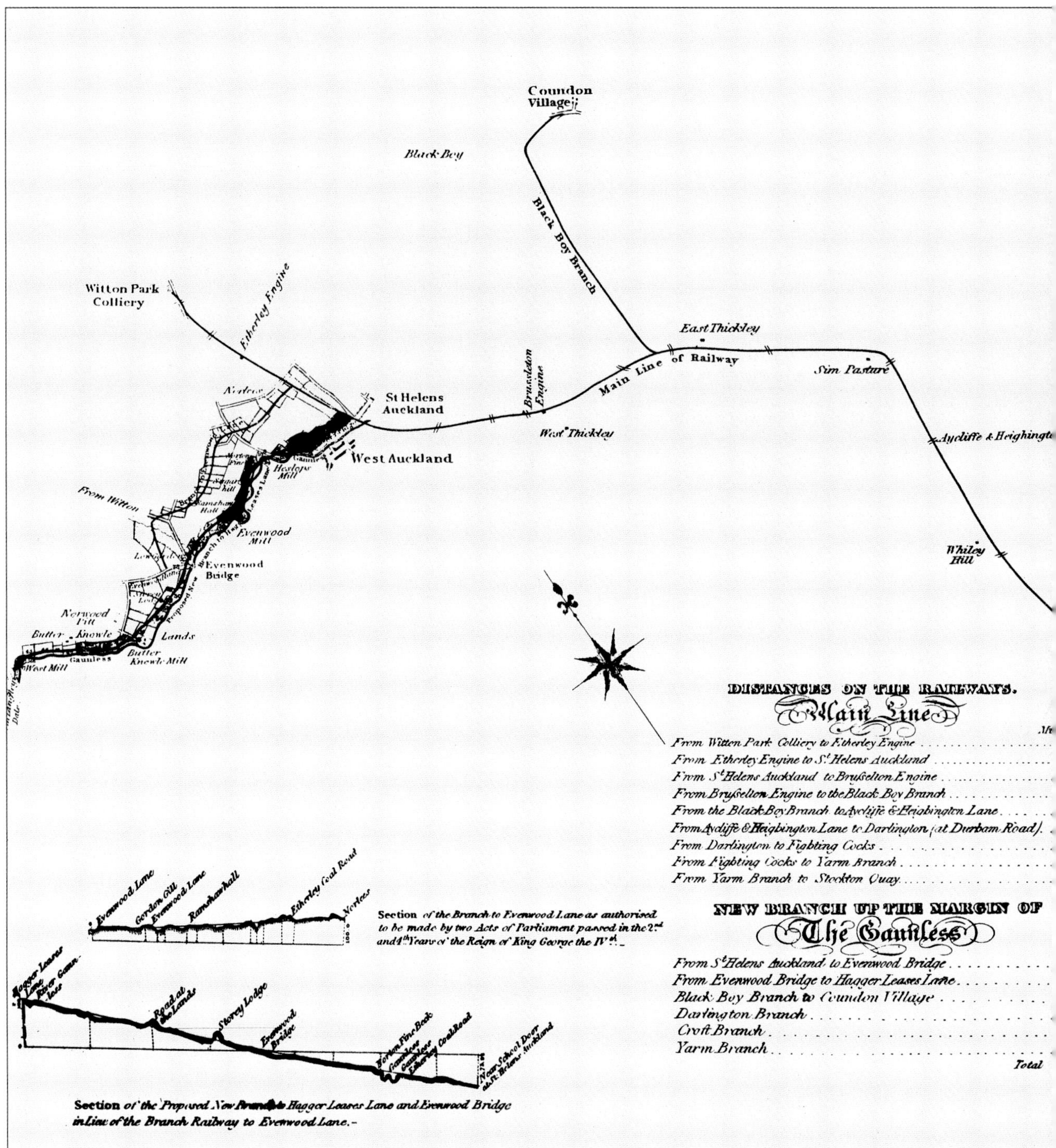

George Stephenson conducted a third survey which included some of Overton's route, mostly at the Stockton end of the line. The authorisation of the third route and George Stephenson's proposals for operating it with inclines and locomotives was

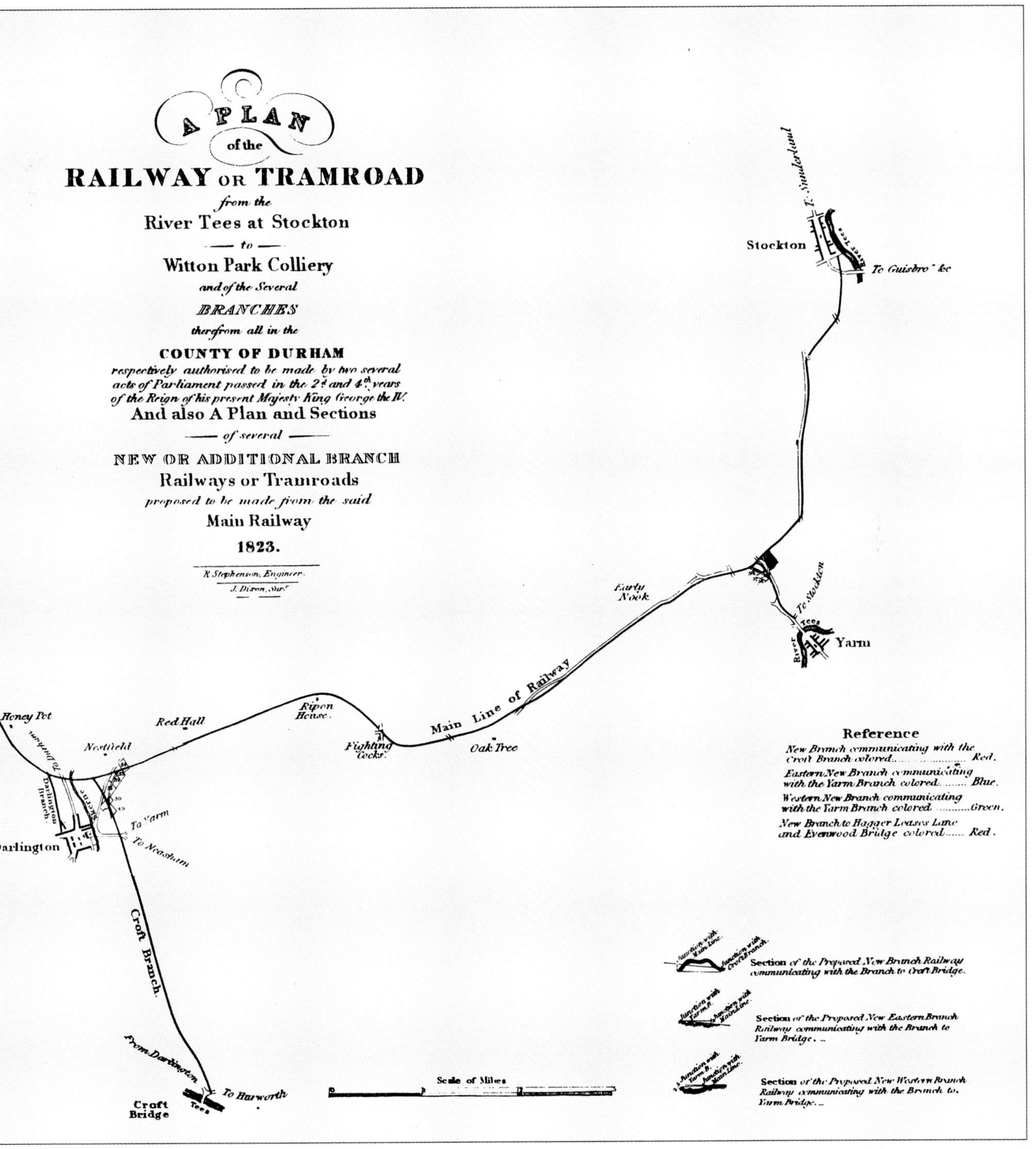

passed by an act of Parliament in 1823. The act also authorised the carriage of passengers. This is the plan of George Stephenson's line.

The sundial on the Stephenson family cottage at Killingworth. When George Stephenson was twenty-four years old the family moved to nearby Killingworth where he worked in Killingworth Colliery with his father. At first his jobs were menial, but as his mechanical talent became evident, he gained quick promotion. By 1812 he was an engine-wright in charge of all the machinery of the 'Grand Allies'.

A painting of the Stephenson family at Killingworth by John Lucas. Their cottage and one of George's locomotives are seen in the background; George and his son Robert are on the right.

This portrait by an unknown English artist is of George Stephenson's son Robert, who was born on 16 October 1803 at Willington Quay, Northumberland. George ensured that Robert received the formal education he had missed and was delighted with his son's high intelligence. While George was working as an engineer on the S&DR, Robert was withdrawn from his job as a pit-viewer to help his father with the line's construction. His name appeared on some of the plans, but his input was limited. It was George who was responsible to the company. Before the line was complete Robert had left for South America to make a new life for himself. He joined an exploratory mining expedition to Mexico, which had been organized by the Quaker businessman Thomas Richardson.

George Stephenson has been called the father of railways, but he alone did not invent them: no man could do that. He established the railway and made it work. In that, he had the invaluable support of other men, the most notable of whom was the devout Quaker, Edward Pease, who is rightly acknowledged as the creator of the S&DR and is seen here in his later years. Born in 1767, Edward Pease was well into his fifties when he became involved in railway construction. He had intended retiring from the family woollen business in 1817 to devote himself to his work as an Elder for the Society of Friends. He became convinced of the need for a tramroad to be built to stimulate trade between Stockton and Darlington. In 1819, together with other business friends, he arranged for a bill to construct a line to be presented to Parliament. It ran into violent opposition from the Duke of Cleveland and was thrown out. In 1819 an alternative route was sanctioned by Parliament. Originally Pease's idea had been for the tramway to be worked by horses. Then, in 1821, George Stephenson suggested to him that the line would be worked more efficiently by steam locomotion and Pease was converted to the idea. He appointed George Stephenson engineer to the project and Stephenson made modifications to the route to make it easier to work with steam locomotion. The first rail was laid on 23 May 1823.

Much of the glory for the S&DR went to the engineers and much of the profit to the entrepreneurs, whereas the vast majority of the work was carried out by the navvies. Using gunpowder, horses, wheelbarrows, picks and shovels these unruly labourers worked dangerously and lived according to their own laws. The first navvies were Lincolnshire fen people, sea-wall builders or 'bankers'. However, later the bulk of the navvies came from Scotland, Ireland and the Yorkshire and Lancashire Dales. They were called 'navvies' or 'navigators' because their background was in canal and road building. They lived in shanty towns, following the route of the line. Many suffered serious accidents and even death as a result of recklessness and drunkenness.

Thomas Meynell, JP of Yarm, one of the promoters of the S&DR and its first Chairman, officially laid the line's first rail on 23 May 1822.

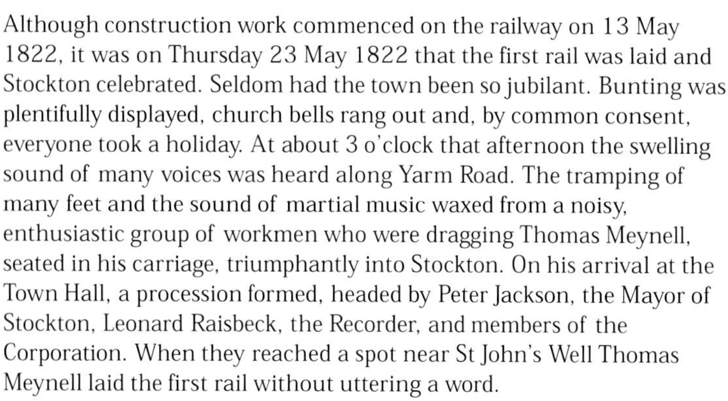

Although construction work commenced on the railway on 13 May 1822, it was on Thursday 23 May 1822 that the first rail was laid and Stockton celebrated. Seldom had the town been so jubilant. Bunting was plentifully displayed, church bells rang out and, by common consent, everyone took a holiday. At about 3 o'clock that afternoon the swelling sound of many voices was heard along Yarm Road. The tramping of many feet and the sound of martial music waxed from a noisy, enthusiastic group of workmen who were dragging Thomas Meynell, seated in his carriage, triumphantly into Stockton. On his arrival at the Town Hall, a procession formed, headed by Peter Jackson, the Mayor of Stockton, Leonard Raisbeck, the Recorder, and members of the Corporation. When they reached a spot near St John's Well Thomas Meynell laid the first rail without uttering a word.

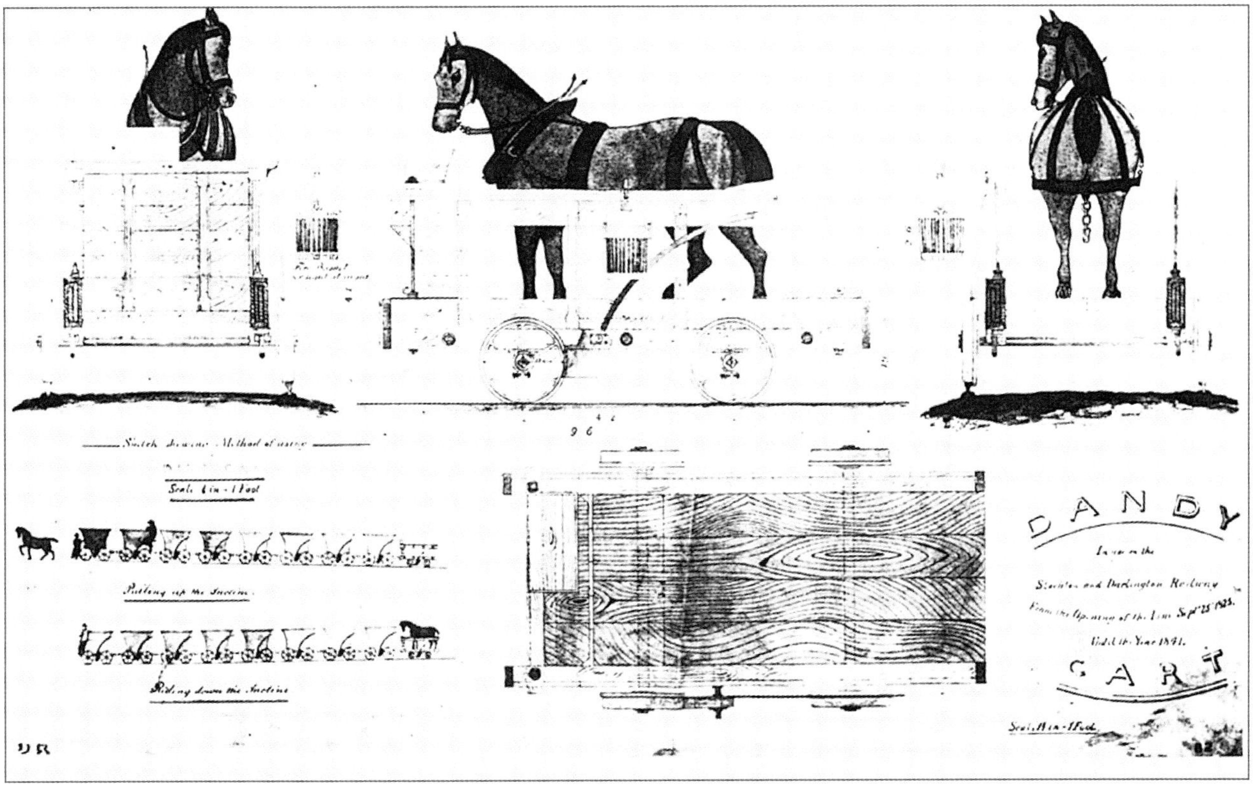

This illustration shows front, side and rear views of a dandy wagon and its use as an early horse box. The S&DR line was 26 miles long, 25 of which were completed by the opening day. At its western end successive pairs of cable-worked inclined planes carried the line over the Etherley and Brusselton ridges, the section between, at West Auckland, being worked by horses. From Shildon the line to Stockton and Darlington was relatively level and here a combination of horses, gravity and locomotive engines were to be employed.

On some inclines, once the horse had pulled loaded wagons to the top, it was usual to disengage it and tether it by a halter to the rear wagon to trot after the descending 'train'. This so shook up the wretched horse that in 1829 a little, light truck, the dandy wagon, seen here, was fastened behind the other wagons so that the horse could gallop up to it and jump in at full speed. There it could eat hay from an attached manger, clearly visible on the right, during the descent. As the wagons slowed the horse was taken from the dandy wagon, rushed ahead of the still moving wagons and attached to the leading one, ready to pull them again. It was estimated that the dandy wagon saved the S&DR more than £1,000 per annum.

On the section of the line from Shildon to Witton Park wagons of coal were drawn over the escarpments by two stationary engines based at Etherley and Brusselton. The engine house at Brusselton is seen here in about 1930 with the top drums in position. The larger one hauled the wagons from the West Auckland valley and the smaller one lowered the wagons to Shildon.

A section of the line from Accommodation Bridge to the west of the Brusselton engine house, *c.* 1930. Stone sleepers carry the line in this photograph, and some of these are still in place. However, they are not the original sleepers laid in 1825, which proved too small to bear the weight of the wagons.

Stone sleepers on the Etherley incline with the stationary engine house in the distance.

Edward Pease, creator of the S&DR, was the line's main financial backer. George Stephenson was born on 9 June 1781 at Wylam, Northumberland, and died on 12 August 1848 at Chesterfield, Derbyshire. He became the most famous character in railway history, was a brilliant engineer and the principal inventor of the railroad locomotive. Michael Longridge was born in 1785, and was one of the founding partners of the Stockton & Darlington Railway Company. He died in Sunderland in 1815. Richard Trevithick was born on 13 April 1771 in Illogan, Cornwall. He constructed the world's first steam locomotive in 1803. He died on 22 April 1833 at Dartford, Kent. Timothy Hackworth was born at Wylam, Northumberland, in 1786. He designed the *Royal George* in 1827. Hackworth was locomotive superintendent for the S&DR and later founded the engine works at Shildon. He died in 1850. Robert Stephenson was born on 16 October 1803 at Willington Quay, Northumberland. He was an outstanding civil engineer and builder of many long-span railroad bridges. He died on 12 October 1859 in London. These men were the cream of the railway pioneers. They were the ones who breathed fire into the S&DR and brought it to life.

THE

STOCKTON & DARLINGTON

RAILWAY COMPANY

Hereby give Notice,

THAT the FORMAL OPENING of their RAILWAY will take place on the 27th instant, as announced in the public Papers.—The Proprietors will assemble at the Permanent Steam Engine, situated below BRUSSELTON TOWER*, *about nine Miles West of* DARLINGTON, *at 8 o'clock, and, after examining their extensive inclined Planes there, will start from the Foot of the* BRUSSELTON *descending Plane, at 9 o'clock, in the following Order:—*

1. THE COMPANY'S LOCOMOTIVE ENGINE.
2. The ENGINE'S TENDER, with Water and Coals.
3. SIX WAGGONS, laden with Coals, Merchandize, &c.
4. The COMMITTEE, and other PROPRIETORS, in the COACH belonging to the COMPANY.
5. SIX WAGGONS, with Seats reserved for STRANGERS.
6. FOURTEEN WAGGONS, for the Conveyance of Workmen and others.

☞ *The WHOLE of the above to proceed to STOCKTON.*

7. SIX WAGGONS, laden with Coals, to leave the Procession at the DARLINGTON BRANCH.
8. SIX WAGGONS, drawn by Horses, for Workmen and others.
9. Ditto Ditto.
10. Ditto Ditto.
11. Ditto Ditto.

The COMPANY'S WORKMEN to leave the Procession at DARLINGTON, and DINE at that Place at ONE o'clock; excepting those to whom Tickets are specially given for YARM, and for whom Conveyances will be provided, on their Arrival at STOCKTON.

TICKETS will be given to the Workmen who are to dine at DARLINGTON, specifying the Houses of Entertainment.

The PROPRIETORS, and such of the NOBILITY and GENTRY as may honour them with their Company, will DINE precisely at THREE o'clock, at the TOWN-HALL, STOCKTON.—Such of the Party as may incline to return to DARLINGTON that Evening, will find Conveyances in waiting for their Accommodation, to start from the COMPANY'S WHARF there precisely at SEVEN o'clock.

The COMPANY take this Opportunity of enjoining on all their WORK-PEOPLE that Attention to *Sobriety* and *Decorum* which they have hitherto had the Pleasure of observing.

The COMMITTEE give this PUBLIC NOTICE, that all Persons who shall ride upon, or by the sides of, the RAILWAY, on Horseback, will incur the Penalties imposed by the Acts of Parliament passed relative to this RAILWAY.

* Any Individuals desirous of seeing the Train of Waggons descending the inclined Plane from ETHERLEY, and in Progress to BRUSSELTON, may have an Opportunity of so doing, by being on the RAILWAY at ST. HELEN'S AUCKLAND not later than Half-past Seven o'clock.

RAILWAY-OFFICE, *Sept. 19th*, 1825.

ATKINSON's Office, High-Row, Darlington.

Ready for the off! Notice issued by the Stockton & Darlington Railway detailing the official opening of the line, including the vehicles that would travel and where they would stop, 1825.

CHAPTER TWO

The Opening

The Loughborough & Nanpantan, opened in 1788, was the world's first public railway; the first steam railway was the Pen-y-Darren Colliery line, which carried VIP passengers at its opening. In 1806 the Swansea & Mumbles became the first passenger railway, and the railway with the distinction of being the first one to be instituted by an act of Parliament was the Middleton Railway, Leeds, in 1758. But the S&DR was the first railway to be worked by steam, although for several years following the gala opening of 1825 its steam traction was reserved for freight. This famous painting of *Locomotion No. 1* pulling some thirty-eight chaldrons and the very first passenger coach 'Experiment' over the Skerne Bridge at Darlington during the opening of the S&DR was based on a contemporary sketch which was altered slightly to show the second 'Experiment', not the first one. Despite that, the picture captures the spirit of the event.

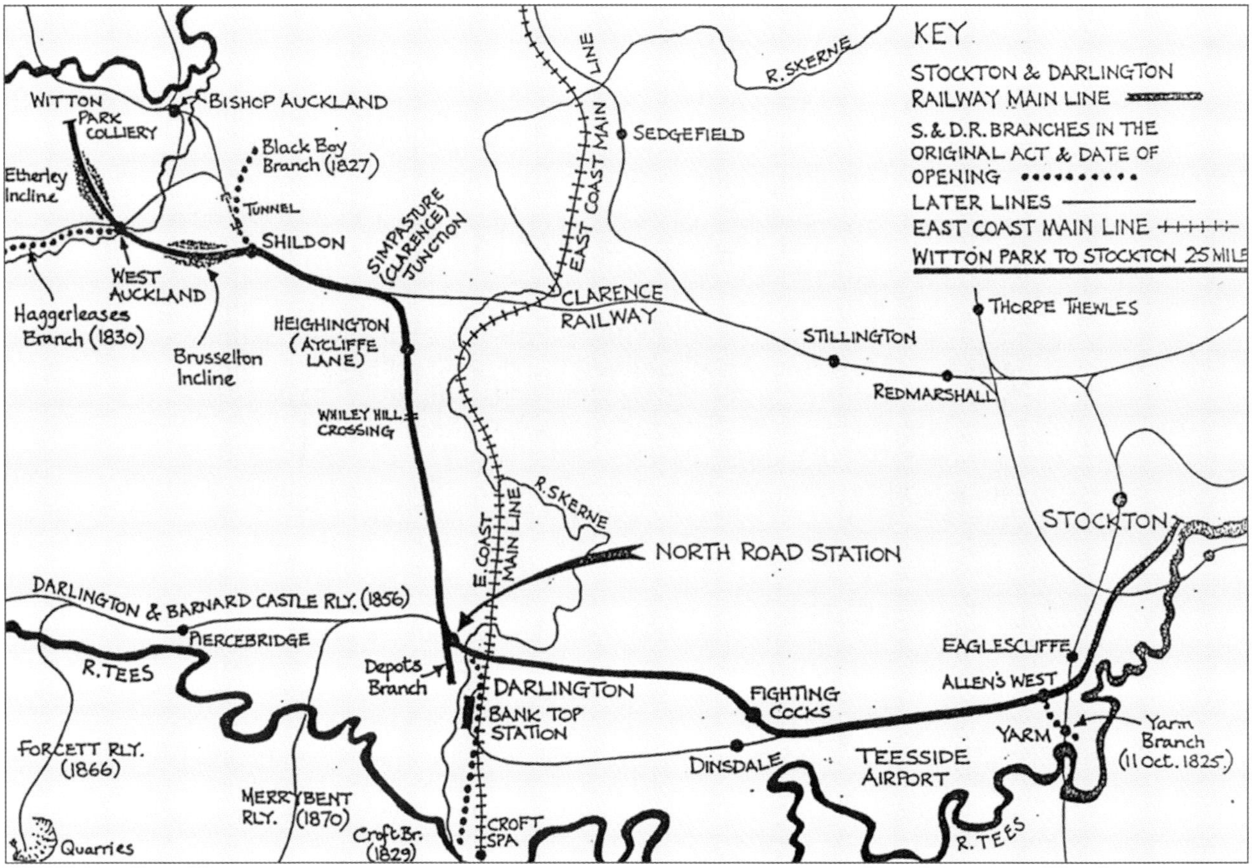

The original railway was nothing more than a line of rails running between hedges and fences through a dozen cuttings and a similar number of embankments from Shildon to Stockton, as this map shows. There were sidings every quarter of a mile, watering places here and there, a few bridges over the rails and one bridge across the River Skerne over which the railway passed. There were coal and lime depots, but that was all. There were no stations, no platforms, no signals, nothing but the line and sidings. However, in 1833 a goods warehouse was transformed into a booking office, waiting room and cottage together with a narrow wooden platform. This served as Darlington's station until 1842 when the North Road station replaced it. Bank Top station was built in 1887.

A Stockton & Darlington Railway Company seal, which would have been used to seal company documents.

More than twenty years before *Locomotion No. 1* there had been many experiments with stationary steam engines and steam locomotives like *Puffing Billy*, seen here outside the Stephensons' cottage at Wylam. Built by William Hedley to his own design, *Puffing Billy* was a relatively large locomotive weighing about 8 tons and, for the most part, Timothy Hackworth, the foreman smith, and Jonathan Foster, principal engineer-wright at Wylam Colliery, did the construction work. It was driven through overhead rocking beams, connecting rods and cranks to gears that drove the four unflanged wheels, designed for plateway track. *Puffing Billy* was the first locomotive to run with a smooth wheel rail and the first to run as a commercial success. William Hedley's experiments inspired George Stephenson to design and build his own locomotives, which were destined to make him world famous.

Locomotion No. 1, preceded by a flag-waving man on a horse, 27 September 1825. The engine is on its inaugural journey from the foot of Brusselton incline to Stockton, pulling the engine's tender, six wagons of coals and merchandise, the Company coach carrying the committee and other proprietors, six wagons with seats reserved for strangers and fourteen wagons for the conveyance of workers.

During the late summer of 1825 the long-expected *Locomotion No. 1* arrived at Aycliffe level carried on a trolley. The whole population turned out to see it and was disappointed. People exclaimed in disbelief, 'This is the iron horse! Why, it's nothing but a steam engine set on wheels.' When *Locomotion No. 1* was placed on the rails at Aycliffe level, the boiler filled with water and wood and coal made ready for lighting, it was discovered that no one had a light and matches were virtually unheard of. George Stephenson was about to send a man to Aycliffe for a lighted lantern when Robert Metcalfe, a navvy, stepped forward and gave him a burning glass, saying that as he, Metcalfe, always lit his pipe with it, perhaps it might fire the engine. Stephenson invited him to try. Using the burning glass and a piece of tarred oakum, Metcalfe lit the fire of *Locomotion No. 1*.

A coach, built at Newcastle to the order of the Stockton & Darlington Company, was delivered on 20 September 1825. It was the first passenger coach ever built, a long one with doors at each end, three windows on each side and a table down the middle. Called 'Experiment', it was constructed to carry sixteen to eighteen passengers sitting face to face along the sides and intended to travel daily between Darlington and Stockton. It was coupled to *Locomotion No. 1* at Shildon and on the evening of 26 September 1825 several members of the committee had a ride in it from Shildon to Darlington, thereby travelling in the first passenger carriage ever seen on a railway. They were Edward Pease Senior, Edward Pease Junior, Joseph Pease, Henry Pease, Thomas Richardson, William Kitching and George Stephenson, whose brother James drove the engine.

From as early as 5.30 a.m. on 27 September 1825 a number of wagons fitted with seats left Darlington for Shildon. Most of the Stockton & Darlington committee, accompanied by friends, set off by road to Bishop Auckland, travelling, for the most part, by post-chaise. On reaching West Auckland they found a scene 'surpassing anything that had ever occurred in that district before'. Crowds were entering the village from all directions, many of them hostile because steam was something that they did not understand. First, committee members inspected the Etherley incline and its stationary engine. Then they examined thirteen wagons, twelve loaded with coals and one with flour, at the foot of Brusselton Bank. At 8 a.m. a 'patent' rope a mile and a quarter long was attached to the wagons and the two 30hp engines at the Brusselton Hill top hauled them to the summit and then lowered them down the other side. At the bottom of the incline, close to where this plaque is sited, bright as a pin with a fresh coat of paint, *Locomotion No. 1* was getting up steam, waiting for the train to be made up.

This plaque was fixed to the world's first railway ticket office in Stockton, the eastern end of the S&DR destination, on Tuesday 27 September 1825. The train halted for half an hour in Darlington where six wagons of coals and twenty-four with workmen separated from the others. The remainder of the procession comprising 6 wagons of coals, 1 wagon of flour, the Company's coach, 20 wagons containing strangers and workmen and Mr Meynell's band, occupying 2 wagons, all drawn by *Locomotion No. 1* proceeded towards Stockton followed by other wagons drawn by horses. While running alongside the turnpike road, the train passed the Stockton-bound stage-coach, drawn by four horses and carrying sixteen passengers, and for a short distance the two ran side by side. On its arrival at Stockton at 3.45 p.m. a salute of seven guns was fired at the Company's wharf and Meynell's band immediately struck up 'God Save the King'.

This is the world's first railway ticket office at Stockton. The distance to it from Brusselton engine is 20½ miles and the entire length of the line from Witton Park Colliery is almost 25 miles, the largest railroad in the kingdom in 1825. No fewer than 40,000 to 50,000 people turned out to see the remarkable events of Tuesday 27 September 1825.

RAPID, SAFE, AND CHEAP TRAVELLING

By the Elegant NEW RAILWAY COACH,

THE UNION,

Which will COMMENCE RUNNING on the STOCKTON and DARLINGTON RAILWAY, on MONDAY the 16th day of October, 1826,

And will call at Yarm, and pass within a mile of Middleton Spa, on its way from Stockton to Darlington, and *vice versa.*

FARES. Inside 1½d.—Outside, 1d. per Mile. Parcels in proportion.

No gratuities expected by the Guard or Coachman.

N. B. The Proprietors will not be accountable for any Parcel of more than £5. value, unless entered and paid for accordingly.

The UNION will run from the Black Lion Hotel and New Inn, Stockton, to the New Inn, Yarm, and to the Black Swan Inn, near the Croft Branch, Darlington; at each of which Inns passengers and parcels are booked, and the times of starting may be ascertained, as also at the Union Inn, Yarm, and Talbot Inn, Darlington.

On the 19th and 20th of October, the Fair Days at Yarm, the Union will leave Darlington at six in the morning for Yarm, and will leave Yarm for Darlington again at six in the evening; in the intermediate time, each day, it will ply constantly between Stockton and Yarm, leaving each place every half hour.

ARCHIVE TEACHING UNIT: THE STOCKTON AND DARLINGTON RAILWAY 1825 27

The first railway journey might have ended, but the celebrations continued unabated. The proprietors of the S&DR, delighted with their success, dined with their friends at the Town's House where 102 gentlemen sat down to an excellent dinner. Fine wines flowed freely and the company did not disperse until 11 p.m. By an ironic twist of fate Edward Pease, who, more than anyone else, had brought the S&DR to fruition, was absent from the festivities because his son, in his early twenties, had died. The whole Pease family was in mourning and kept away.

Most of the S&DR was laid with flexible, 'fish-bellied' iron rails 2½ in wide at the top and 15 ft long. It was George Stephenson, 'Geordie Stivvie' as the locals called him, who advised using malleable iron because, as he put it, 'cast iron will not stand the weight, there is no wear in them [the rails], and you will be at no end for repairs'. The directors decided upon the extensive use of stone blocks for sleepers. While working on the Killingworth wagonway, 'Stivvie' built his early colliery railways to a 4 ft 8 in gauge. The S&DR retained this dimension until 1840 when, for some still obscure reason, another ½ in was added, although none of the rolling-stock needed to be altered because of this. Other early railways used gauges varying between 4 ft 8 in and 4 ft 9 in for many years. The use of horses had its own problems. So that the animals could work comfortably, the rails were supported on stone blocks which left the centre of the track free for the horses to move along.

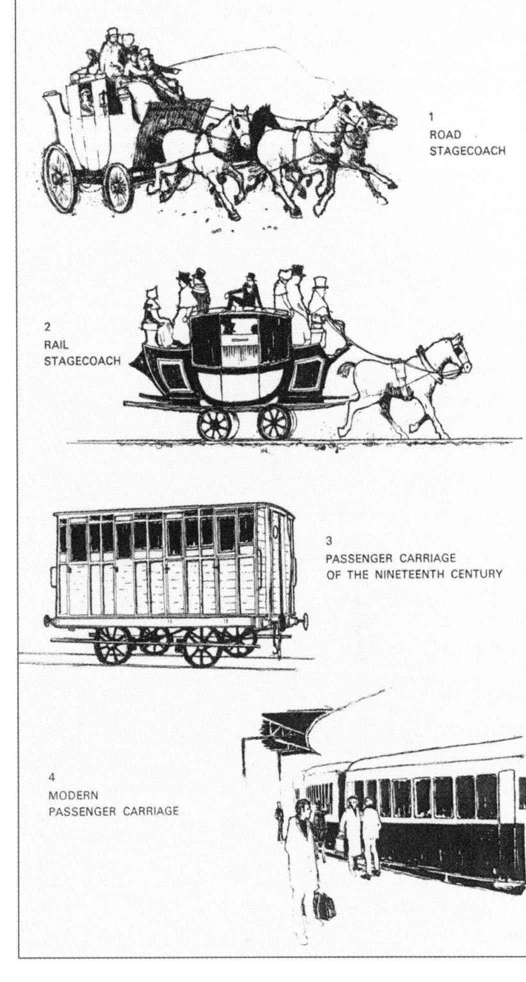

The coach 'Experiment', seen here outside the Fleece Inn, Stockton, first ran between Stockton and Darlington on 10 October 1825. The 'Express' started in 1826 and, to meet the unexpected demand, some old stage-coaches were requisitioned and mounted on flanged wheels. The early coaches were all pulled by a single horse, were all in private hands, the drivers being licensed by the Company to operate under the name. They were private speculators and paid a certain amount to the Company to operate under its name. When coaches and wagons met each other at equal distances from the sidings, of which there were only four between Stockton and Darlington, there were frequent angry confrontations. To obviate these quarrels a post was erected halfway between each siding and the first coach to reach it had the right to proceed over the remaining distance. On rounding corners the coachman blew his horn, a task later adopted by the steam whistle. Coaches never failed to stop to pick up wayside passengers. Fares were collected by the guard *en route*. All the early coaches had a brake, operated by a long handle.

ABSTRACT

Of the Cash Account for the Year ending 30th of June, 1827.

Dr. Jonathan Backhouse, Treasurer, in Account with the Stockton & Darlington Railway Co. Cr.

Dr.	£.	s.	d.
To Cash received in Sundry Loans . .	30,753	11	6
Do. do. on account of Tonnage &c. .	16,876	8	7
Balance due to the Treasurer . .	2,691	1	6
	£.50,321	1	7
Amount of Two Instalments of 20 ℘ Cent. New Share Account . . .	13,000	0	0

Cr.	£.	s.	d.	£.	s.	d.
By Balance due to the Treasurer .				10,459	3	9
Cash paid on account of dividends .				726	1	10
Stephenson & Co. for permanent Engines				4,000	0	0
H. Birkbeck, repayment of his Loan .				1,000	0	0
Interest, Discount, and Commission .				3,371	5	4
Cash paid on account of Land for the Main Line, Croft Branch, Black Boy Branch, and Hagger Leases Branch				4,598	4	2
Newmarch and Co. for Kenton Engine, purchased for Black Boy Branch .				528	4	6
Cash on account of Law Expences				300	0	0
Allowance to Owners of Black Boy Colliery, to the 1st June last, ℘ order of General Meeting . . .				1,037	9	4
Do. to W. L. Wharton, ℘ do. . .				151	13	0
Additional outlay (viz) Depots, Erections, &c. on the Main Line and Branches, Locomotive Engines, &c.				8,698	12	0
Cash paid for sundry Materials and Labour, for Waggons, &c. for increase of Carrying establishment .				3,674	17	5
Sundry contingent Expences (viz) Smith and Wright's Work, Labour, Damages, Freight, Carriage, Agents' and Clerks' Salaries, Rates, Stationary, Travelling Expences, Postages, &c.	4,612	18	4			
The Monthly Pay Bills (viz) Labour and Consumable Articles, at the fixed and Locomotive Engines, and for additional Horses employed in leading Coals and Lime	2,807	7	9			
Do. as under:—						
Repairing the Way & Materials 1818 16 2						
Sundry Contingent Labour 1060 2 4						
Cleaning Cuts and repairing embankments . . 514 15 6						
Repairing Waggons, Engines, &c 527 1 7						
Leading, &c. . . . . 434 8 7—	4355	4	2—	11,775	10	3
				£.50,321	1	7
Balance				2,691	1	6

Receipts for Tonnage, &c.

	Coals.				Lime.				Lead, Timber, Iron, and Merchandize.				Coaches.				Sundry Tonnage and Sale of Bricks.			Total.		
	Tons.	£.	s.	d	*Tons.*	£.	s.	d.	*Tons.*	£.	s.	d.	*Miles.*	£.	s.	d.	£.	s.	d.	£.	s.	d.
1826 *July*	4814	1014	4	6	662	75	16	7	1008¼	92	7	9	3972	49	13	1	129	12	0	1361	13	11
August	3719	587	17	0	343¼	41	14	4	1170¼	115	9	5	4588	64	2	0	29	9	10	838	12	7
September	7999¾	1520	4	2	817¼	115	2	9	927½	96	10	10	4448	61	18	0	309	0	11	2102	16	8
October	7562¾	1336	2	5	532	54	1	11	1181¾	112	13	4½	5844	73	1	0	189	3	1	1765	1	9½
November	6666¾	1152	11	9	239¼	25	5	4	1176¼	118	9	7½	4098	51	4	6	87	13	4	1435	4	6½
December	4945¾	1027	10	5	99¼	21	15	6	1079½	103	17	7	3156	39	13	0	2	8	1	1195	4	7
1827 *January*	3532½	705	13	2	53¾	4	18	11	870	79	9	9	2506	28	13	4	51	10	1	870	5	3
February	5766¾	1044	17	6	181¼	10	0	7	1036¼	96	14	7	2722	30	11	2	49	1	9	1231	5	7
March	7279¾	1420	17	3	211¾	38	18	0	898	89	8	8	3064	34	14	0	43	0	6	1626	18	5
April	7707¾	1267	10	11	976¾	128	2	1	1121	109	6	0	3262	37	4	8	120	5	4	1662	9	0
May	10412¾	1649	6	8	2054	247	9	5	1259¾	119	6	8	3920	45	4	2	6	18	7	2068	5	6
June	10041	1728	9	5	2075	263	11	5	1116¼	106	9	10	3880	47	15	10	0	0	0	2147	17	11
	80,446*	14455	5	2	8,246¾	1026	16	10	12,846¼	1240	4	1	45460	563	14	9	1018	3	6	18,305	15	9

**Of which 18,588 Tons were exported, 26,385 do. sold at Darlington, 10,560 do. at Yarm, 21,866 do. at Stockton.*

FIRST PRINTED STATEMENT OF RAILWAY ACCOUNTS.

With the opening of the S&DR coal poured into Stockton quicker than it could be cleared, and it was soon realized that accommodation provided for coal was insufficient. Long lines of coal wagons crowded the railway for 2 miles from the Stockton staiths. Something had to be done. Darlington men believed in extending the railway to a point further down the river while Stockton men believed in making another cut at Portract which would allow ships to come up river more easily. This abstract of the cash account for the year ending 30 June 1827 and the receipts for tonnage for the 1826–7 period highlight the problem. Between July 1826 and June 1827 the amount of coals and lime alone carried on the S&DR had increased tremendously, causing a permanent bottleneck at the Stockton end of the line that had to be remedied.

Stockton and Darlington RAILWAY.

Rates of TONNAGE,

On the Main Line of Railway, Black Boy, Darlington, Yarm, and Croft Branch RAILWAYS.

	s.	d.	
For all Coal, Cinders, Ashlar, and Hewn Stone, Slate, Marl, Sand, Lime, Clay, and other Minerals; also Bricks, Tiles, Lead, in Pigs or Sheets, Bark, Timber, and all sorts of Manure, the Sum of	0	1½	Per Ton per Mile.
For Meal, Flour, Grain, Straw, and Hay, Bar and Pig Iron, Staves and Deals, the Sum of .	0	2	Per Ton per Mile.
For all Goods, Commodities, and Merchandize, not above specified, the Sum of . .	0	3	Per Ton per Mile.
For Ditto, Ditto, deposited in any Warehouse, or on any Wharf, or Landing-Place, belonging to the Company, the Sum of	0	1	Per Ton for the space of 48 hours, and 2d. per Ton for every further 7 days, for Warehousing.
For all the Articles, Matters, and Things, for which a Tonnage is herein-before directed to be paid, which shall come upon the Inclined Planes, on the Main Line, worked by the Permanent Engines, the Sum of	0	6	Per Ton for each Engine.
For all Coal, Lime, and Stone, which shall be Shipped on Board of any Vessel or Vessels, in the Port of Stockton-upon-Tees, for the purpose of Exportation, the Sum of . .	0	0½	Per Ton per Mile.
For all Coal, Lime, or Stone, Shipped on Board any Vessel or Vessels, in the Port of Stockton-upon-Tees, to be delivered at Saltburn or Hartlepool, the Sum of . . .	0	1	Per Ton per Mile.
For all Stones and Gravel to be used for the making or repairing Public or Private Roads, the Sum of	0	0½	Per Ton per Mile.
For all rough Ruble Stone, for the purpose of Building, the Sum of . .	0	1	Per Ton per Mile.
For Spoutage and Labour of all Coals and Lime, Shipped from the Company's Wharfs, the sum of	0	2	Per Ton.
For Coal, Lime, and Stone, or other Materials, deposited at any of the Shoots, or Depots, (exclusive of those at Darlington, Croft, Yarm, and Stockton,) formed and erected by the Company, the sum of	0	1	Per Ton.
For Haulage of Coals, and use of the Company's Waggons, for Home Consumption, the sum of	0	0½	Per Ton per Mile.
For Ditto of Lime and Stone, Ditto, Ditto, the sum of	0	0⅝	Per Ton per Mile.
For Haulage of Coals, Lime, and Stone, and use of the Company's Waggons, for Exportation, the sum of	0	0¾	Per Ton per Mile,
For every Chariot, Coach, Chaise, Car, Gig, Landau, Waggon, or other Carriage, which shall be used for the Conveyance of Passengers, ~~to and from~~ Darlington, ~~Croft~~, Yarm, and Stockton, on all days in the Week, (Sundays excepted,) the sum of . . .	0	3	Per Mile.
For Ditto, Ditto, between Darlington and Witton-Park, the sum of .	0	1½	Per Mile
For Ditto, Ditto, which shall be used for the Conveyance of Passengers on Sundays . .			Double Toll.
For Dttio, Ditto, which shall be used for the Conveyance of Passengers, and shall come upon the Inclined Planes, worked or not worked by the Permanent Engines, the sum of . .	1	6	Each Plane,
For all Articles, Matters, and Things, for which a Tonnage is herein-before directed to be paid, ascending the Northern or Southern Planes, on the Black-Boy Branch, or any part thereof, the sum of	0	6	Per Ton.
For all Articles, Matters, and Things, for which a Tonnage is herein-before directed to be paid, descending the Northern or Southern Planes, on the Black Boy Branch, and which shall not have ascended, the sum of	0	2	Per Ton.
For Weighing all Coal, Cinders, Stone, Lime, and other Minerals; Depot Rents, Laborage, keeping Accounts, and Collecting Monies at the Croft Depots, and Paying the same Weekly to the Owner or Owners, or such other Person as he or they may appoint, the sum of .	0	5	Per Ton.

Percival Tully, *Collector*, at Darlington.
George Applegarth, *Ditto*, at Stockton.

1st *October*, 1829.

At a meeting in Darlington in November 1818 Edward Pease had told a highly respectable audience that he was confident that the proposed S&DR would produce a modest but sure financial return. By 1 October 1829 results had exceeded his wildest dreams, and by 1825 receipts had quadrupled and were continuing to rise. In the 1830s the S&DR line was doubled from Brusselton Bank to Stockton and trade once again expanded dramatically. This poster details tonnage rates in 1829, which have increased somewhat over the years as the pound has lost its value.

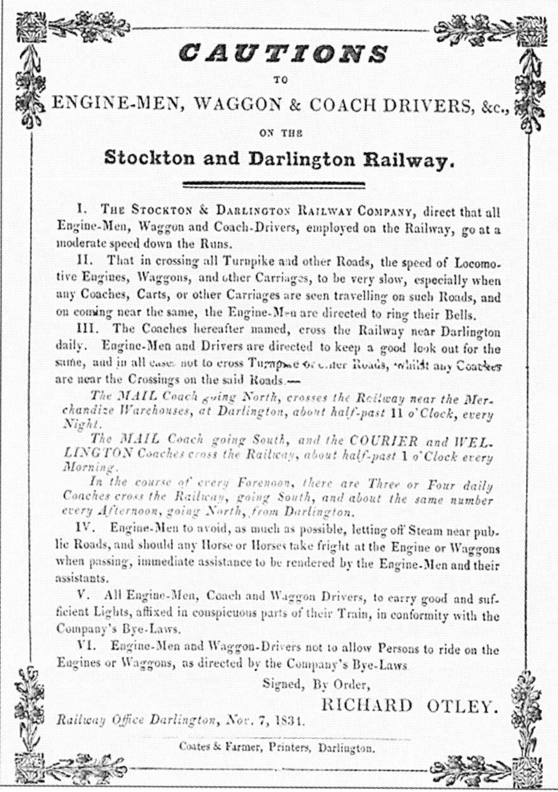

CAUTIONS

TO

ENGINE-MEN, WAGGON & COACH DRIVERS, &c.,

ON THE

Stockton and Darlington Railway.

I. THE STOCKTON & DARLINGTON RAILWAY COMPANY, direct that all Engine-Men, Waggon and Coach-Drivers, employed on the Railway, go at a moderate speed down the Runs.

II. That in crossing all Turnpike and other Roads, the speed of Locomotive Engines, Waggons, and other Carriages, to be very slow, especially when any Coaches, Carts, or other Carriages are seen travelling on such Roads, and on coming near the same, the Engine-Men are directed to ring their Bells.

III. The Coaches hereafter named, cross the Railway near Darlington daily. Engine-Men and Drivers are directed to keep a good look out for the same, and in all cases not to cross Turnpike or other Roads, whilst any Coaches are near the Crossings on the said Roads.—

The MAIL Coach going North, crosses the Railway near the Merchandize Warehouses, at Darlington, about half-past 11 o'Clock, every Night.

The MAIL Coach going South, and the COURIER and WELLINGTON Coaches cross the Railway, about half-past 1 o'Clock every Morning.

In the course of every Forenoon, there are Three or Four daily Coaches cross the Railway, going South, and about the same number every Afternoon, going North, from Darlington.

IV. Engine-Men to avoid, as much as possible, letting off Steam near public Roads, and should any Horse or Horses take fright at the Engine or Waggons when passing, immediate assistance to be rendered by the Engine-Men and their assistants.

V. All Engine-Men, Coach and Waggon Drivers, to carry good and sufficient Lights, affixed in conspicuous parts of their Train, in conformity with the Company's Bye-Laws.

VI. Engine-Men and Waggon-Drivers not to allow Persons to ride on the Engines or Waggons, as directed by the Company's Bye-Laws

Signed, By Order,

RICHARD OTLEY.

Railway Office Darlington, Nov. 7, 1831.

Coates & Farmer, Printers, Darlington.

This notice from 1831 explains that the north and south-going mail coaches have priority at the turnpikes. Also, engine-men are to avoid letting off steam near public roads so as not to frighten the horses.

This bell, inscribed 'S&D Railway 1833', was once rung to mark the beginning and end of shifts on the railway.

CHAPTER THREE

The Early Years

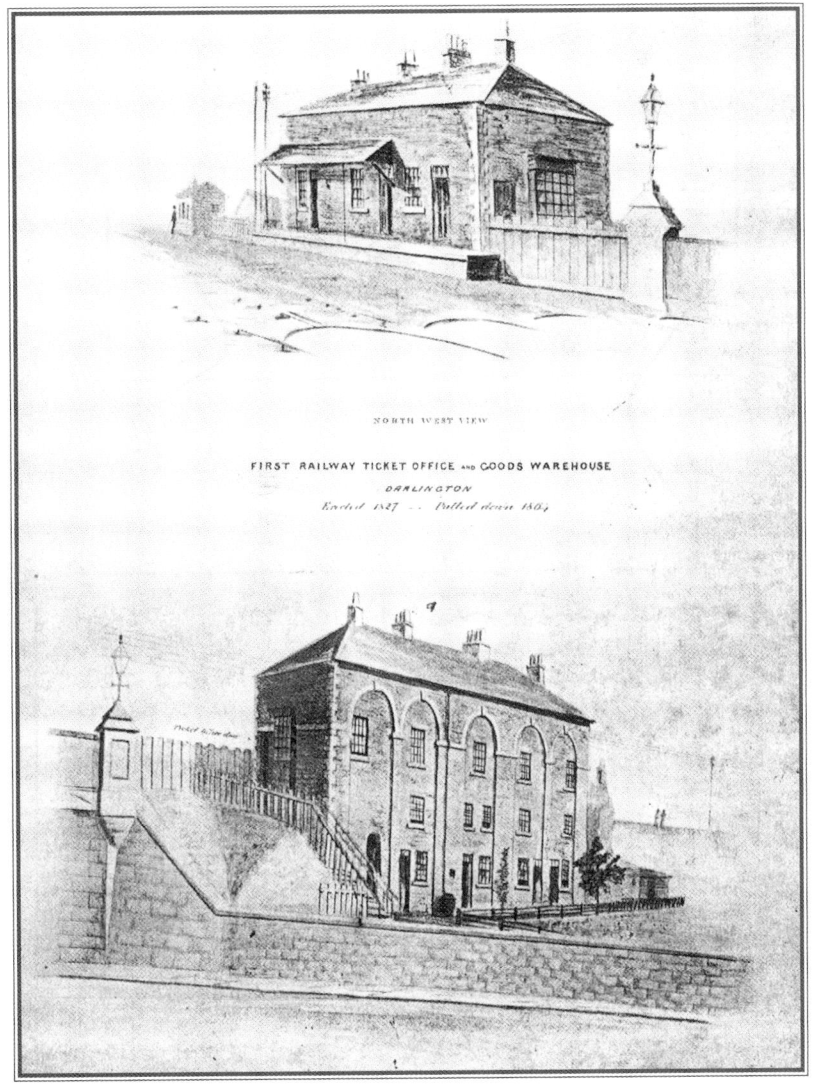

This station, which sufficed for Darlington from 1833 to 1842, was actually a small goods warehouse comprising a booking office, waiting room and cottage, with a narrow wooden platform approached by a flight of steps from the east side of the North Road near the Skerne Bridge. It was replaced by a new North Road station, which became the Darlington Railway Museum in 1975. It is not sited on North Road itself but is west of it and is believed to be the oldest railway station in the world.

Darlington North Road station was opened by the S&DR in 1842 because the Company felt that it needed a proper station in one of the principal towns it served. It was eventually eclipsed by Darlington Bank Top station and became the railway museum, apart from one platform that is an unstaffed halt. The museum's most notable exhibit is *Locomotion No. 1*.

When William Lister's Iron Foundry was established in 1830, a siding from the adjoining S&DR was laid into it. These pieces of cast-iron rail and the stone blocks on to which they were fixed were found in 1952 during excavations and are seen here at an S&DR exhibition in Darlington, 1975.

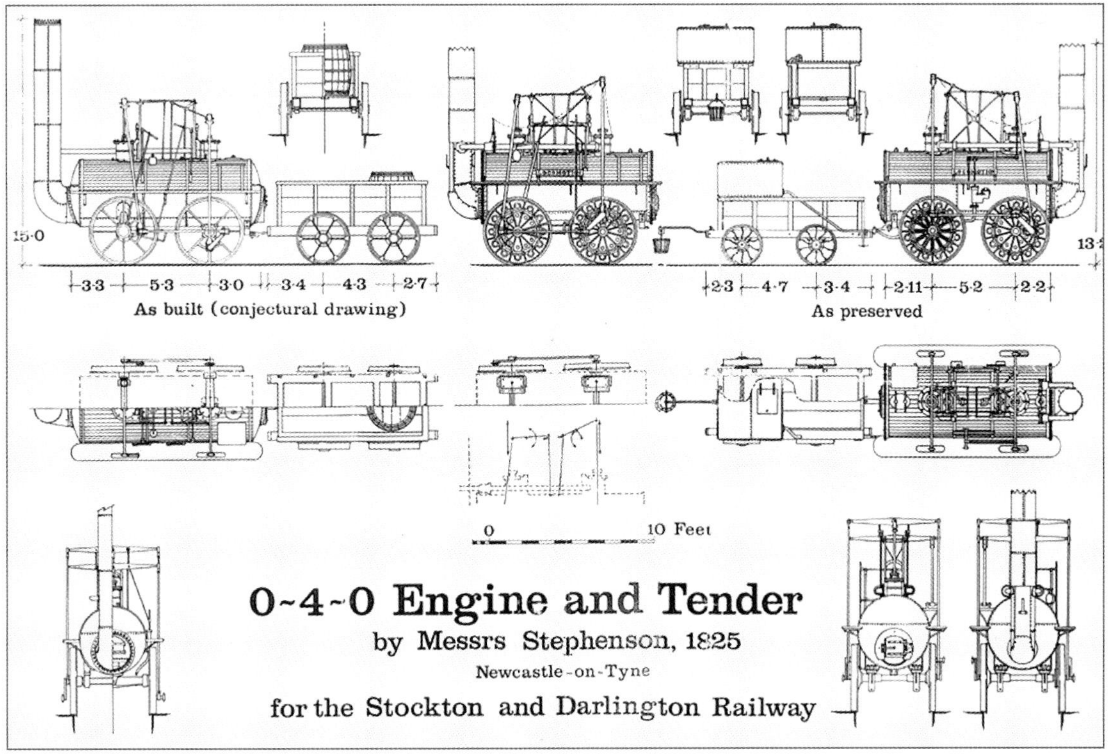

The S&DR's first locomotive *Locomotion No. 1* was built under George Stephenson's direction by Robert Stephenson and Co. at their Forth Street Engine Works, Newcastle. In Robert Stephenson's absence Timothy Hackworth came from Wylam to supervise its construction. This done, he returned, briefly, to Wylam before moving to Shildon to take charge of the S&DR's stationary engines and locomotives. From these drawings the differences between the locomotives, as built, and as preserved, are clear.

The S&DR was a huge success from its opening. Timothy Hackworth, the engineer responsible for the day-to-day running of the line, was hard pressed to improve the often inadequate performance of *Locomotion No. 1* and the Company's three other locomotives. *Locomotion No. 1* was the first locomotive to have its wheels coupled by rods, as is shown in this photograph of its replica at Beamish Open Air Museum in 1975. Thanks to Hackworth's constant maintenance, *Locomotion No. 1* ran regularly between Darlington and Stockton carrying 450 passengers at 15mph, thus living up to its original name *Active*. At the side to the rear of the tender there was a danger signal, an iron-barred receptacle filled with coal which, when lit, acted as a warning before the advent of the oil lamp. The first signal employed on the S&DR was an ordinary fire grate that swung suspended from a coach or a wagon, glowing like a red coal in the distance, but smoking and crackling when stationary. Along the whole of the S&DR in 1825 there was not a single lamp.

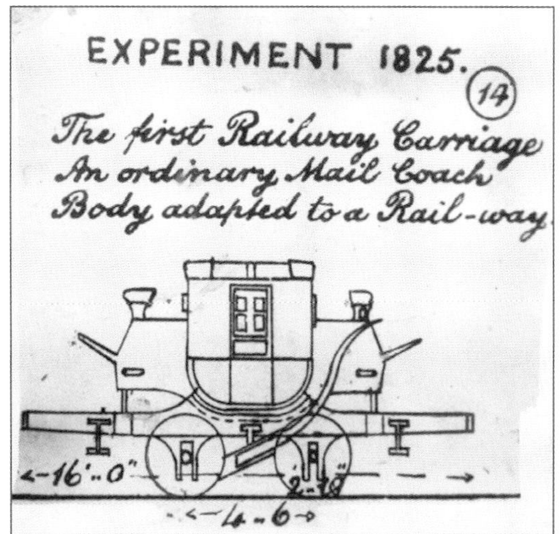

This is a drawing of one of the old stage-coaches requisitioned by the S&DR to meet demand; it is called 'Experiment' after the first purpose-built railway coach. It was mounted on flanged wheels, which were welded to the axle, and this increased the friction when the wheels were in motion. Many carriages had open tops and passengers had to contend with sparks and hot cinders whenever firemen stoked the engine. Open carriages had a short life and were followed by covered carriages which had seats lengthways on each side with a double row along the middle with passengers sitting back to back. So loudly did the windows and doors rattle when the train was in motion that it was difficult for passengers to hear each other speak.

The next style of carriage had about three compartments, the back of each compartment being just above the heads of the passengers. Someone at one end of the carriage wishing to be near a friend at the opposite end would climb on to the seats and go over the compartments much to the dismay of the other passengers. Further improvements followed when the back of each compartment was raised to the top of the carriage so that each compartment was self-contained. This S&DR coach was in use between 1840 and 1850. The roof rail on top indicates that the passenger luggage was carried on the roof. The coach design is similar to that of a stage-coach. There is a second-class compartment at each end with first class in the middle.

On 27 October 1829 the Croft Branch of the S&DR was opened and on 1 January 1831 amid great rejoicings the Middlesbrough Branch was also opened and a double line was laid. A suspension bridge, seen here, was built across the River Tees at Stockton by Samuel Brown Esq. It was 274 ft long, 25 ft broad and 60 ft high and calculated to sustain a weight of 150 tons. On arriving at the suspension bridge on opening day, the railway coaches carrying the Company from Darlington were joined by their colleagues from Stockton and all proceeded to Middlesbrough where they were received with the firing of guns and great demonstrations of joy. One train driver, dubious about the stability of the suspension bridge and believing strongly in self preservation, reduced speed as the engine approached it, jumped off the engine and ran ahead of it. At the far side he stepped back on to the engine and continued the journey. In 1844 this bridge was replaced with a new one because the suspension bridge could not cope with the increased and heavier traffic. On 4 June 1846 the Redcar to Middlesbrough Railway was opened. During the celebrations *Locomotion No. 1* travelled the 7½ miles in 25 minutes.

Jane Hackworth stands near the Shildon tunnel entrance looking at the original plans. In 1839 the proprietors of the S&DR began constructing Shildon tunnel so as to obviate the disadvantages attendant on the use of the Brusselton and Black Boy inclines. The tunnel, almost ¾ mile long, took twenty-one months to build. During its formation the tunnel was worked by seven shafts from its surface. It is 23 ft 4 in high, 21 ft wide to the beginning of the arch and at its deepest it is 120 ft underground.

STOCKTON AND DARLINGTON RAILWAY COACHES.

WINTER OF 1837-38.

ST HELEN'S AUCKLAND TO DARLINGTON.		DARLINGTON TO ST HELEN'S AUCKLAND.	
First Trip	at half past 8 o'clock.	First Trip	at 8 o'clock.
Second do.	half past 12 "	Second do.	quarter past 12 "
Third do.	at 5 "	Third do.	quarter before 5 "

N B.—The Train will leave Shildon a quarter of an hour after leaving St Helen's Auckland. A CAR from Bishop-Auckland to St Helen's, meets each of these trains in going and returning. An extra Coach will leave Darlington for St Helen's Auckland, on Mondays, Tuesdays, and Fridays, at 2 o'clock in the afternoon.

DARLINGTON TO STOCKTON.		STOCKTON TO DARLINGTON.	
Second class Train	at half-past 6 o'clock.	First class Train	at quarter past 7 o'clock.
First class do.	quarter past 9 "	Second class do.	at 9 "
Second class do.	at 11 "	First class do.	half past 11 "
First class do.	half past 1 "	Second class do.	half past 1 "
Second class do	half past 3 "	First class do.	at 4 "
First class do.	at 6 "	Second class do.	at 6 "

The Darlington Trains, both going and returning, are in immediate connexion with the Middlesbrough Trains.

STOCKTON TO MIDDLESBROUGH.		MIDDLESBROUGH TO STOCKTON.	
First Trip	at 8 o'clock.	First Trip	at 7 o'clock.
Second do.	at 9 "	Second do.	half past 8 "
Third do.	at 10 "	Third do.	half past 9 "
Fourth do.	half past 12 "	Fourth do.	quarter past 11 "
Fifth do	quarter past 2 "	Fifth do.	at 1 "
Sixth do.	at 3 "	Sixth do.	quarter before 3 "
Seventh do.	at 5 "	Seventh do.	quarter before 4 "
Eighth do.	quarter before 7 "	Eighth do.	half past 5 "

The Company's Clocks are invariably kept with those of the General Post Office, London, which time may be seen at Mr HARRISON'S, Clock Maker, High Row, Darlington.

N.B.—Tickets must be taken at least Five Minutes before the time of Starting.

Passengers for the EXMOUTH COACH (going to Lancaster) must leave Stockton by the 4 o'clock, and Darlington by the quarter before 5 o'clock, Train; returning, the EXMOUTH is in time for the half past 8 o'clock Train from St Helen's Auckland.

A COACH will leave DARLINGTON for CROFT at a quarter past 9, and at half past 1 o'clock.

MARKET COACH.

A Coach and Cattle Carriage will leave St Helen's Auckland on MONDAYS at half past 6 o'clock, and Shildon at 7 in the Morning.

All Parcels (requiring haste and care) are to be left as under, 15 Minutes before the Trains start.

John Proud, Bishop Auckland.	Sarah Pearson, Glass Warehouse, Darlington.
John Coxon, St Helen's Auckland.	John Simpson, Majestic Office, Stockton.
Robert Thompson, New Shildon.	John Unthank, Middlesbrough.

This winter timetable of 1837–8 refers to locomotive-driven railway coaches. On 7 September 1833 the S&DR began to substitute locomotives in lieu of horse-drawn coaches for all passenger traffic between Stockton and Darlington.

Stockton and Darlington Railway,

Statement of Work done and Expenses Working and Repairing Locomotive Engines from July 1st 1838, to the 30th June 1839.

Coal and Merchandise Department.

No. of Engine.	Name.	Tons hauled.	Tons hauled over one Mile.	Train Miles run.	Cost of Repairs. £ s. d.	Coal, Stores & Enginemen's Wages. £ s. d.	Interest on Value of Engine. £ s. d.	Total Working Cost. £ s. d.	Cost per Ton per Mile in pence. d.	Cost per Train Mile in pence. d.
1	Locomotion.	17.136	326.180	9.854	195 17 3	197 3 11	14 13 4	407 14 6	.300	9.93
2	Hope.	31.940	680.441	17.182	330 16 11	368 2 7	32 10 .	731 9 6	.258	10.21
3	Black Diamond	14.082	255.333	6.474	734 . .	127 0 7	2 10 .	863 10 7	.811	32.01
4	Diligence.	35.416	743.325	19.950	387 2 10	406 13 1	36 5 .	830 0 11	.268	9.98
5	Royal George.	28.481	608.720	15.332	373 4 11	327 2 11	25 . .	725 7 10	.286	11.35
6	Experiment.	17.155	244.096	7.454	135 0 6	152 2 3	19 . .	306 2 9	.301	9.85
7	Rocket.	4.009	51.913	884	17 3 2	26 14 4	1 6 8	45 4 2	.209	12.27
8	Victory.	27.421	599.741	16.385	485 13 3	326 9 7	20 . .	832 2 10	.333	12.18
9	William 4th.	2.597	60.133	1.760	28 2 1	33 11 11	26 10 .	90 4 .	.360	12.30
10	Planet.	"	"	.	. . .	. . .	. . .	. . .	.	.
11	Beehive.	36.987	842.465	21.200	373 9 11	452 5 10	41 5 .	867 0 9	.247	9.81
12	Majestic.	"	"	.	. . .	. . .	20 . .	20 . .	.	"
13	Coronation.	24.274	435.664	14.019	201 3 7	254 12 7	19 15 10	475 12 .	.262	8.14
14	Tees.	41.848	967.475	24.628	408 12 5	516 7 1	42 10 .	967 9 6	.240	9.42
15	Tory.	17.222	372.409	9.809	209 18 5	199 9 3	29 15 .	439 2 8	.283	10.74
16	Director.	30.439	676.443	18.243	297 16 10	384 0 4	42 10 .	724 7 2	.257	9.52
17	Whig.	12.758	286.328	7.569	84 14 1	148 16 8	17 . .	250 10 9	.210	7.94
18	Shildon.	6.748	153.852	5.297	105 17 8	89 9 3	26 9 2	221 16 1	.346	10.05
19	Darlington.	22.257	489.017	13.939	385 16 8	262 15 1	34 . .	682 11 9	.335	11.75
20	Adelaide.	39.222	887.208	23.912	373 4 11	489 18 11	42 10 .	905 13 10	.245	9.09
21	Earl Grey.	39.503	874.469	22.313	306 5 9	495 0 8	44 . .	845 6 5	.232	9.09
22	Lord Durham	36.635	743.329	18.879	313 8 10	397 13 7	41 10 .	752 12 5	.243	9.56
23	Wilberforce.	44.494	635.522	16.688	318 10 8	353 12 8	37 10 .	709 13 4	.268	10.20
24	Magnet.	29.146	335.136	18.832	324 12 6	401 15 6	50 . .	776 8 .	.556	9.89
25	Enterprise	32.545	669.876	16.926	523 17 4	366 10 11	36 5 .	926 13 3	.332	13.14
	Briton.	37.087	675.992	22.031	225 19 4	454 3 2	43 15 .	723 7 6	.257	7.88
	Totals.	623.402	12615.067	349.560	7140 9 10	7233 12 8	746 10 .	15.120 12 6	.287	10.38

Coaching Department.

	Train Miles		Working Cost.
Planet	7172		209 3 8
Swift	8342		243 6 2
Arrow	10530		307 2 6
Sunbeam	28224		823 4 .
Queen	6789		198 0 3
Totals.	61,057	at 7d per mile	1780 16 7

The Coach Train Engines were maintained by Engine Builders who were Contractors and were paid at the rate of 7d. per Train Mile.

(Signed.) John Graham.

On this annual statement for the year 1 July 1838 to 30 June 1839, all twenty-five of the engines working on the S&DR are named and their costs detailed.

From hauling the first passenger train in the world on 27 September 1825, *Locomotion No. 1* continued to serve the S&DR until 1841. In 1835 it won a race with a mail coach by 100 yd over 4 miles. It ended its useful life at Messrs Pease and Partners West Collieries, South Durham, as a pumping engine. In 1857 it was put on display at Darlington North Road station, was subsequently shown at many exhibitions, took part in the railway centenary celebrations of 1925 and is now based at the Darlington Railway Museum. The top sketch shows *Locomotion No. 1* in 1866; the bottom one shows High Row, Darlington, and the town centre before the famous town clock, original town hall and the covered market were built.

The *Derwent* was built by A. Kitchin at Hopetown Railway Foundry, Darlington. After being delivered to the S&DR in November 1845, it ran for many years but was eventually purchased by Messrs Pease and Partners for use on their private lines. It was presented to the North Eastern Railway Co. in 1898 for preservation and exhibition. It also took part in the railway centenary celebration in 1925.

CHAPTER FOUR

The Timothy Hackworth Connection

Timothy Hackworth and the locomotive are synonymous, yet he was a very devout Wesleyan Methodist who shunned publicity. As a result he has not been given credit due to him for his outstanding work in the development of the locomotive. In 1825 Timothy Hackworth had already been appointed Superintendent of Permanent and Locomotive Engines. The eldest son of John Hackworth, he was born at Wylam on 22 December 1786, and was educated at the village school until he was fourteen years old, when he began a seven-year apprenticeship as a blacksmith. He soon found that he had 'a natural bent and aptitude of mind for mechanical construction and research'. In 1816 he was offered employment as foreman smith at Walbottle, where he remained for eight years. William Patter, the manager, was a man of high character, and a close friendship developed between himself and Timothy Hackworth, which lasted throughout their lives. During his happy years at Walbottle, many changes took place in the construction of railroads, although no improvements were made to locomotives, none of which was of any concern to him. In 1823 George Stephenson opened a small factory at Forth Street, Newcastle, under the name of Robert Stephenson and Co. and was soon supplying the railway with ironwork. Timothy Hackworth was offered the post of manager, which he declined, but when George Stephenson was compelled to leave Newcastle for some months surveying the Liverpool & Manchester Railway, and again asked Hackworth to become temporary manager, he accepted. When, towards the end of 1824, George Stephenson returned from his surveying duties, he was so impressed with the efficient manner in which the coach works had been conducted during his absence that he was determined to retain Timothy Hackworth's services. He offered him one half of his own interest in the business. Without giving reasons, Timothy Hackworth declined the offer. Such was the measure of the man.

In the minutes of the committee of management of the S&DR dated 13 May 1825 the following appointment is recorded: 'John Dixon' – who assisted George Stephenson in making the survey of the original S&DR and who dealt with that important undertaking's details – 'reports that he has arranged with Timothy Hackworth to come and settle on the line, particularly to have the superintendence of the permanent and locomotive engines. The preliminary arrangement as regards salary is £150 per annum, the company to find a house and pay for his house – rent and fire.' This is how Timothy Hackworth came to live in New Shildon where he was much involved with the affairs of the first public railway until his death on 7 July 1850.

Soho Works was built on a wet, swampy field, home to snipes and peewits, near the ancient township of Shildon. It was chosen because its position below the Brusselton incline marked the place where locomotives ceased and the inclined plane began. It was a depressing area that had sprung up entirely because of the coming of the railway. Its development lacked the orderly planning of a township and it simply grew as buildings were needed, being entirely an industrial centre. The site comprised a railway repair shop, a barnlike building divided into a joiner's shop and a blacksmith's shop with two smith's hearths, and a small engine shed, seen here in 1975, with room for only two locomotives.

Locomotive No. 1 was the only locomotive from Stephenson's Newcastle factory working on the line throughout 1825. It was an unfortunate engine. It had difficulty making steam and could pull a maximum of only eight wagons. Within a month of working the line it broke a wheel. Then, on 1 July 1828, it blew up on Aycliffe Lane, killing the driver, John Cree, and maiming the water pumper, Edward Turnbull. Timothy Hackworth had the unenviable task of repairing it. The only tools Hackworth had available to him were basic, as this photograph of original tools from the New Shildon Sheds shows.

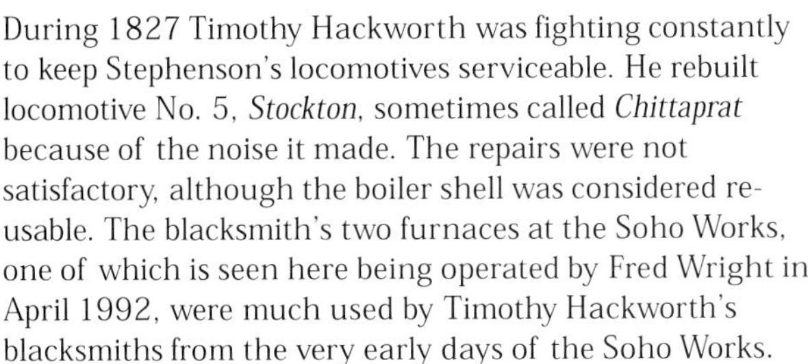

During 1827 Timothy Hackworth was fighting constantly to keep Stephenson's locomotives serviceable. He rebuilt locomotive No. 5, *Stockton*, sometimes called *Chittaprat* because of the noise it made. The repairs were not satisfactory, although the boiler shell was considered re-usable. The blacksmith's two furnaces at the Soho Works, one of which is seen here being operated by Fred Wright in April 1992, were much used by Timothy Hackworth's blacksmiths from the very early days of the Soho Works.

Modelled on the original and correct in most respects, this is Timothy Hackworth's first locomotive of his own design, the *Royal George*. Within five months of its triumphal opening, events exposed waning confidence and disappointed hopes in the S&DR. Even George Stephenson fell from favour and Edward Pease tried to withdraw from the Forth Street locomotive works at Newcastle, which 'was by no means in a prosperous state'. The subscribed capital of the Company was £67,500. By the end of May 1826 £86,895 in extra money had been borrowed and there were unpaid debts of £15,000 including £5,000 owing to Robert Stephenson and Co. Many of the lenders were clamouring for their money. Capital and loans were all spent, the branch lines that formed part of the original scheme were still unmade and an attempt to raise a new loan failed. The Company was unable to pay current expenses and share prices fell. At the dinner in Stockton on the evening of the opening day shares were at a premium of £40 – 'Plenty of purchasers but no sellers'. Now there were plenty of sellers but no buyers. The S&DR was going through a most critical period. The Company had to employ additional horses to increase trade and improve returns which the committee had been reluctant to do because this reflected badly on the locomotives. When Timothy Hackworth proposed to construct an engine suitable for working traffic, he was requested to attend a meeting convened for the purpose of discussing the future of the S&DR. When asked for his opinion he replied, 'Gentlemen, if you will allow me to make you an engine in my own way I will engage that it shall answer your purpose'. The committee agreed to his proposal. No man had more experience of locomotives and he had staked his reputation on the project. The committee left the matter in his hands and the result was the famous engine the *Royal George*.

The *Royal George* was technically a great advance on previous designs. The mass of spidery rods and levers, the hallmark of the primitive engines, had gone. At 15 tons, it weighed almost twice as much as *Locomotion No. 1*, which weighed only 8 tons, and the weight was spread over six wheels. The driving axle was rigid with the boiler, the other two axles being sprung and the wheels coupled by rods outside the wheels. It had a feed water heater by which fresh water was heated by the exhaust steam before it was pumped into the boiler. The exhaust was turned up the chimney to form the blast pipe which induced air through making it burn brightly. The use of the return flue in the boiler was a reversion to Hackworth's earliest design. In this the flue in which the fire burned doubled back inside the boiler so that the chimney was at the same end but alongside the fire. The return flue gave twice the area for heat to be transferred from the fire to the water. It also meant that the driver could be at one end of the locomotive and the fireman at the other. Another Hackworth speciality was a coal and water wagon, known later as a tender, which was attached at either end of the locomotive.

Hackworth's spring-loaded safety valve ensured that the boiler pressure, still about 50lb per square in or 3½ atmospheres, did not exceed a safe limit. It was a great improvement on the mechanism that was first used, which consisted of a weight on the end of a lever that held down a valve. These valves would release steam unnecessarily when the engine ran over bumps in the track. The valves could be held down unofficially by hand or with extra weights, causing excessive pressure to build up which frequently resulted in the boiler exploding, usually with fatal consequences.

Timothy Hackworth's residence at New Shildon, where he lived from 1833 until 1850, known as Soho House, though the family preferred to call it Soho Cottage. He was never happier than when there, acting host, meeting and entertaining, as he frequently did, men of high position in the scientific world. His relationship with his business associates was generally harmonious with one exception. In his early days some friction, soon forgotten, arose between Thomas Storey, a surveyor, and himself. Storey lived at West Auckland and Hackworth at New Shildon. Both had to attend committee meetings at Darlington on Fridays. A horse-drawn stage-coach on railway wheels was used to convey passengers and when it arrived at New Shildon from West Auckland, en route to Darlington, if Storey was on top, Hackworth invariably got inside. If Storey was inside, Hackworth would go on top, even if the weather was wet and stormy.

This view of one of the bedrooms in Soho House shows what an unpretentious but comfortable home it was, similar to thousands of others throughout England. Everything about the house was spotless, Timothy Hackworth placing cleanliness next to godliness. He had a fondness for fine glassware, china, silver plate and spotless table linen. The furniture was in the solid style of the day and his books were equally substantial: the family Bible, Bunyan's *Pilgrim's Progress*, an early edition of *Encyclopaedia Britannica*, Wesley's *Sermons* and, in a lighter vein, Byron's poems and the works of Sir Walter Scott. Timothy Hackworth was a patriot, proud of the British Constitution. All his children were brought up to fear God and honour the King. He enjoyed singing north-country ballads and songs. He detested working on Sundays and his works were always closed from Saturday until Monday, no matter how pressing the business. Yet Sundays held no rest for himself. He was a local preacher on the Barnard Castle circuit and preached twice, sometimes three times on any Sunday. In his early days he had been an expert dancer, at that time a recreation not approved of by Methodists. Music was also one of his pleasures, a subject in which his daughters were instructed.

As the engineer responsible for the day-to-day running of the S&DR Timothy Hackworth had all his work cut out improving the often inadequate performances of *Locomotion No. 1* and its three fellow locomotives *Hope*, *Black Diamond* and *Diligence*. When it was decided to erect engine-building shops in Whessoe Road, Darlington, the district became known as 'Hope Town' after the locomotive *Hope*. The first tender of *Locomotion No. 1* carried a large wooden water barrel. It was made by Darlington cooper Mason Brotherton at his Blackwellgate workshop and was so large it had to be assembled in the street outside his workshop. Drivers of all early nineteenth-century engines like *Locomotion No. 1* would stand or sit on a plank at the side of the boiler, as seen here on this model, with the fireman at the back to fire the furnace. A recent £5 note shows *Locomotion No. 1* speeding across a bridge with both driver and fireman at the rear, leaving no one to drive the train.

The S&DR attracted passengers in their thousands and carried coal by the hundreds of thousands of tons. One local businessman, a Mr Lambton, did a deal with the S&DR whereby coal due to be sent onwards by ship would be charged at the rate of only a halfpenny per ton per mile whereas coal for local use was charged at 4 pence per ton per mile. This low and seemingly ruinous rate demonstrated that the economic potential of this new means of transport was sound. Soon the line was carrying half a million tons of coal annually, fifty times the anticipated figure. In 1830 Timothy Hackworth persuaded the S&DR management committee to embark on a programme of expansion, and of the twenty-three engines that were delivered, seventeen were based on an improved version of the *Royal George*. In late 1830 he got approval for two new designs, both developed at New Shildon. They were for a 'Director' class, 0–6–0 engine. No. 13 of this class became *Coronation*, seen here in this 1930s LNER advertisement. In May 1833 there was a collision between *Coronation* and *Lord Durham* at Urlay Nook, and in October of that year *Coronation* was in collision with wagons in Bowesfield Lane, Stockton, and by October 1840 it was beyond repair.

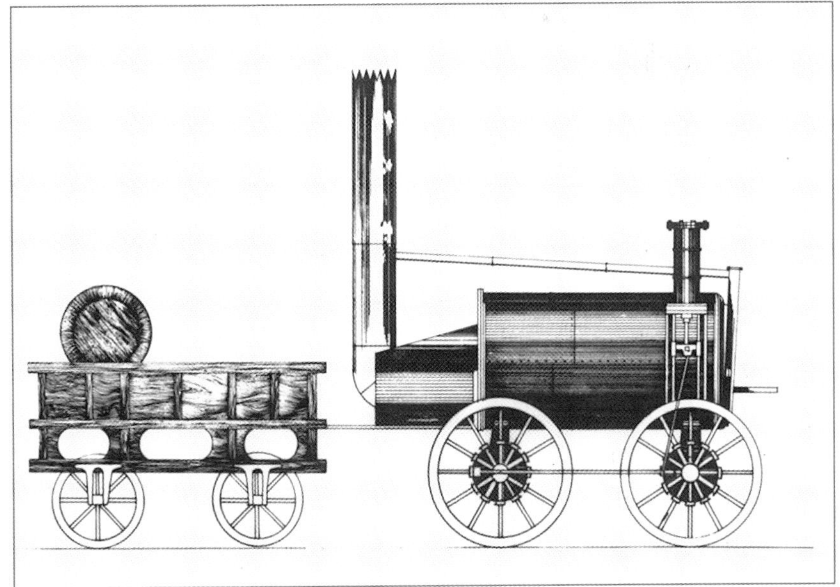

A drawing of Thomas Hackworth's locomotive *Sanspareil*. The Rainhill Trials, which began on 6 October 1829, to promote a locomotive that was lighter, faster, more powerful and more reliable than those in general use, attracted both Timothy Hackworth with *Sanspareil* (Without Equal) and Robert Stephenson with the *Rocket*. In total there were five entries for the competition and a prize of £500 was offered for a locomotive that met all the conditions. The *Sanspareil* was 5cwt over the stipulated 4½ tons for a four-wheeled locomotive and was disqualified. However, the judges decided to put the engine through the same trial 'as if it conformed to the proposed conditions to see if its performance would be favourable to the Directors'. It soon became clear that it was a powerful competitor. At its top speed it travelled a mile in 4 minutes 17 seconds, a rate of 15mph. However, boiler leakage due to inferior workmanship resulted in delays. Then one of the cylinders, supplied by Robert Stephenson, burst. Under these circumstances the *Sanspareil* stood little chance against the *Rocket*, which was perfect in all construction details.

Jack Wright surveys some original railway line unearthed at the Soho Works, New Shildon, in July 1992.

Throughout the building of the *Rocket*, Robert Stephenson regarded the *Sanspareil* as a serious rival. His efforts to keep down the *Rocket*'s weight paid off and its official weight was recorded as 4 tons 5cwt. Its great advantage was a separate firebox and small copper fire tubes immersed horizontally in its boiler, dividing the air and increasing the heating surface. At the Rainhill Trials the *Rocket* was the only engine to conform strictly to the conditions and even these were modified at the last moment.

Laying track on the original S&DR at New Shildon, January 1993. Until 1833 the coaching trade on the S&DR was carried out by different proprietors independently of the Company, using horse-pulled coaches. Then the Company began to find that it would be more advantageous if it took the whole trade into its own hands and replaced horses with steam locomotion. By that time traffic had become heavier and the track began to suffer. The original track consisted of rails that were held in chairs that were pinned to square stone sleepers. Heavier locomotives tended to cause the rails to spread, which sometimes resulted in derailments. With steam locomotives, the need for an obstacle-free gauge between the rails to accommodate the horses no longer applied. Now wooden sleepers stretching across the gauge prevented the rails from spreading.

Ladies wearing clothes that were in vogue during Timothy Hackworth's happy years at Soho House. When he and his small staff started the New Shildon shops in 1826 there was no place of worship. Timothy Hackworth had been brought up in the Church of England but had converted to Methodism before he settled at New Shildon. He immediately set aside a room in his house for worship, but it soon became too small. By 1829, through his exertions, a Methodist chapel was erected in Shildon and, in 1831, another was built in New Shildon. Mrs Hackworth, a tall handsome woman of great individuality and competence, supported him to the hilt. They had a large family with six daughters and two sons. A third son died in infancy. Mrs Hackworth survived her husband by two years and died in 1852.

Two central figures in Timothy Hackworth's work were William Bouch, Senior Partner at Shildon Works Co. and John Graham, who joined the S&DR in 1831. His role encompassed the duties of station master, clerk and mineral agent. He became General Superintendent in 1831, a position he held until he left the Company in 1849.

CHAPTER FIVE

Shildon Works

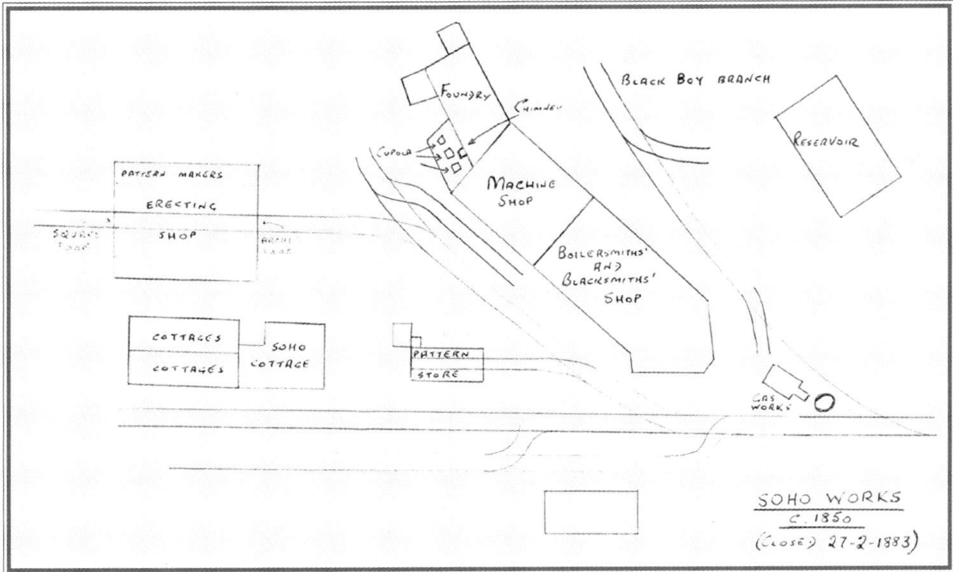

The Soho Works, *c.* 1850. As one of the pioneers of locomotives, Timothy Hackworth always kept at the forefront of development. However, finding his activities in this respect limited for what was by the standards of the day now a small railway, he resigned from the S&DR in 1840 to devote all his time to his private factory at Soho Works, New Shildon. Seven years earlier, in 1833, he had founded the works here, putting his brother Thomas in charge. When Timothy Hackworth left the S&DR his place as the Company's engineer was taken by William Bouch who held the position for the rest of the railway's separate existence. Five years after Timothy Hackworth's death in 1850, his Soho Works was acquired by the S&DR and was used as an extension of the main Shildon Works until 1883, when it closed.

Soho Work's main building, *c.* 1900. The foundry chimney, left, machine shop, centre, and the boilersmiths' and blacksmiths' shop, right, are seen here. This building was demolished in 1946.

The west end of the Soho Works. It grew to about 6 acres in the decade between 1840 and 1850 and had a branch line connecting directly with the S&DR. At the north end there were coal-drying ovens and an iron foundry. To the south there were blacksmiths' and boilersmiths' shops together with warehouses, stores, the pattern shop, offices, a row of workmen's cottages and Timothy Hackworth's own residence. At a later date a separate erecting shop was added, a tall building able to accommodate ten locomotives for construction at any one time. Shildon Works began as the headquarters of the S&DR locomotive department and for many years locomotives in normal running use were housed and maintained there. But the emphasis soon switched to wagon building, and in so doing Shildon Works gained the double distinction of being the oldest main works and the largest and most important wagon works in British Rail.

The S&DR Company established the Shildon Works in 1833 to maintain and build locomotives. This 1960s' aerial view shows the works at their peak. Over the years they were progressively modernized and extended to occupy an area of 55 acres, of which 13 acres were covered workshops. At one time the workforce numbered approximately 2,750.

From the late 1860s Shildon Works had a major responsibility for building and maintaining rolling-stock, many vehicles of new design having been proved and manufactured there. Some are seen in this photograph taken on 21 August 1976.

The past is not forgotten at Shildon Works. Jack Wright, an ex-welder with British Rail, is working on one of the first rail cars ever built, 19 April 1992.

Apprentice fitters Ian Jackson and Peter Bennet at work on the replica of Timothy Hackworth's *Sanspareil* at Shildon Works before the locomotive and tender were painted in readiness for the 150th anniversary of the Liverpool & Manchester Railway in May 1980. The forgings, fabrications and machining were done at Shildon.

Apprentices at Shildon Works, *c.* 1920. It was common at this time for young boys like these to go straight into apprenticeships on leaving school.

A general view of the construction department with high-capacity wagons being built, 1976. They are seen in various stages of completion.

An artisan at work. Tommy Wood on the punching and cropping machine at Shildon Works, 21 August 1976.

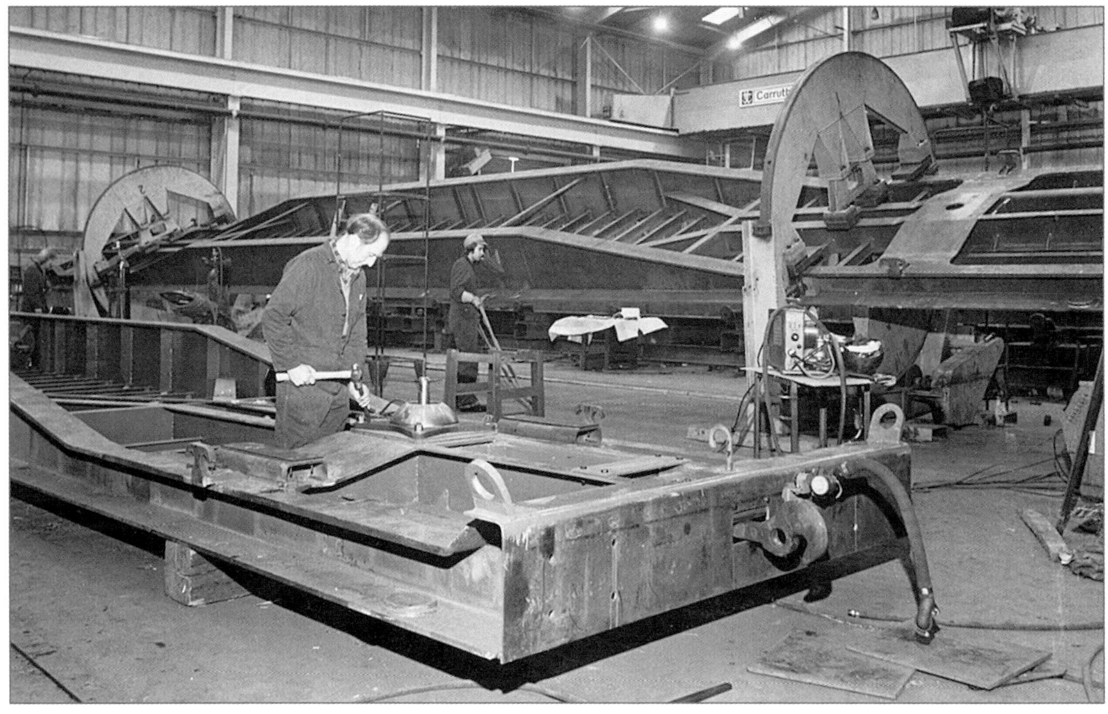

A wagon bogie being assembled, 23 April 1979.

Turning journals and part of a shaft at Shildon Works, 22 July 1954.

The pride on the faces of Works Manager Ian MacDonald's happy team tells of another finished product of which they are justifiably proud, 1977.

The manufacturer's plate on a wagon made at Shildon Works in 1958.

Ever ready to innovate, Shildon Works purchased two 3,000kg capacity Lancer Boss sidelift trucks in July 1978. They reduced the handling time by one-third and increased effective capacity by 50 per cent. The trucks were used for transporting long lengths of steel bar, rolled steel beams and timber from stock to workshops. The previous method involved the use of overhead cranes in conjunction with trailers, which was slow, labour intensive and not without hazard.

Workmen constructing a partly wooden wagon. At the time of nationalization in 1948 British Rail operated a fleet of over a million wagons. Most new mineral and merchandise wagons were constructed with timber bodies and there were many thousands in service with wooden underframes. Since then British Rail policy was to standardize with all-steel construction as far as possible because of the reduced annual maintenance costs and the advantage of increased availability. Timber was only incorporated in the bodies of covered stock and the floors of merchandise and some other open wagons. The use of corrosion-resisting steels and a scheduled programme of scraping and painting provided these wagons with a lifespan equivalent to that of the wooden wagons.

Shildon Works, always synonymous with progress and development, earned a justifiably proud record, constructing new mineral and freight wagons of riveted and welded design and repairing and converting existing wagons and bogie vehicles. A large proportion of drop stampings for other works were also manufactured in the Shildon forge. The repair shops had the capacity for overhauling and repairing up to 800 wagons a week. Not all the new wagons were for the home market. Seen here on 11 November 1970 is the first of 150 bogie pallet wagons ordered by Malayan Railways earlier that year. The contract for the wagons was the first one won by Shildon Works after government permission was given to allow them to tender for private contracts. The wagons came off the production line at the rate of ten per week. They were shipped to Malaya through Middlesbrough Docks.

This new Shildon-built wagon clearly displays the very high quality of workmanship involved in its manufacture, 13 January 1965. The average steel wagon has between 250 and 900 component parts making up its trace weight, each requiring an average of six distinct manufacturing operations.

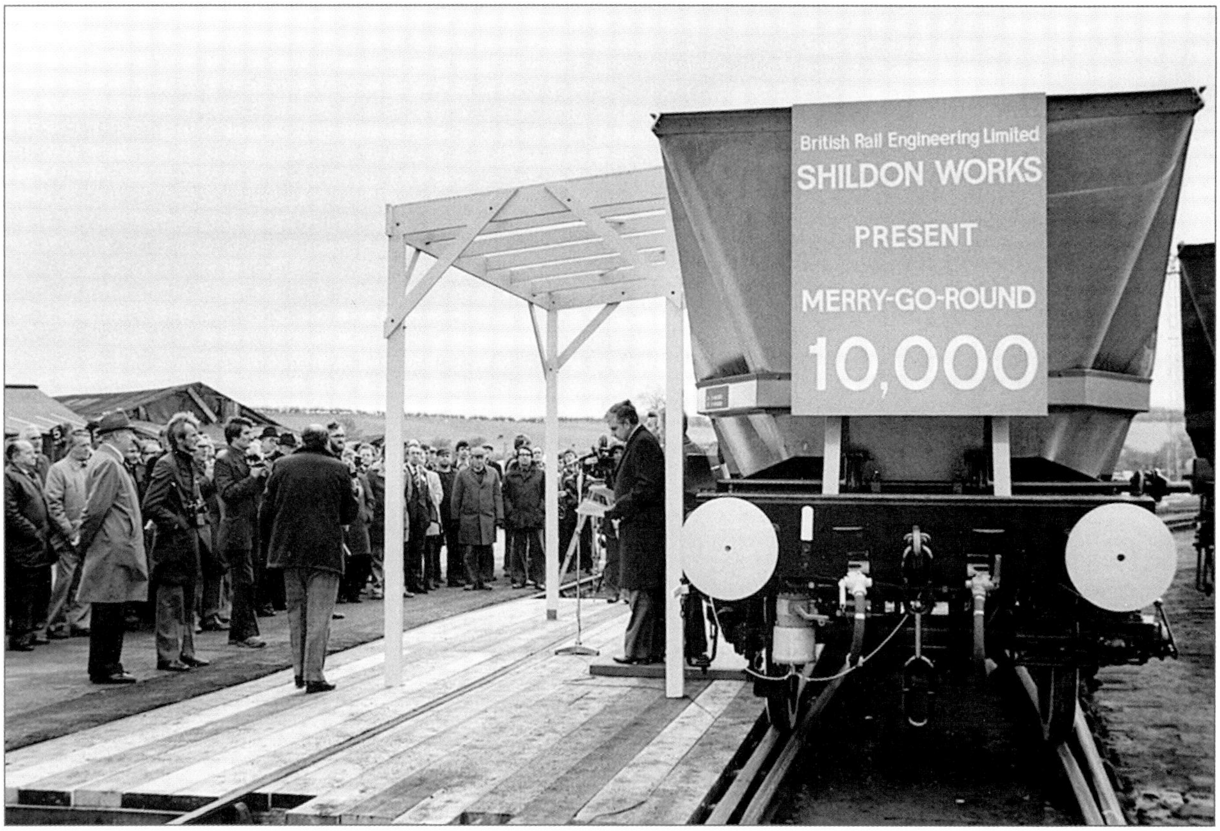

Shildon Works celebrates the completion of the 10,000th 'Merry-go-round' in style, 1980. Between 1965 and 1982 Shildon Works built 11,083 'Merry-go-round' 32.5 tonne capacity coal hoppers with a tare weight of 13 tonnes. The standard wagon frame could be produced as a welded or riveted unit but the former was preferred for its low cost and weight.

'Down a bit . . . left a bit . . . right a bit . . . steady'. A high-capacity wagon being lowered and guided into position on the underframe, 21 August 1976. Shildon Works had an exemplary record of wagon building, achieved by the skill of its craftsmen and the use of modern machines and equipment.

Shildon's commendable record should have saved the works from closure. But the volume of freight traffic transferring from rail to road became so great that by the 1980s the need for new BR freight stock, Shildon's life blood, had largely disappeared. Alarmed, the Shildon workforce and the local townspeople showed their anger and sense of betrayal. Protest demonstrations and mass meetings were held and these were given full coverage by the *Northern Echo* and local television. At this protest, held in May 1983, Ossie O'Brien, far right, and other local MPs give their support.

A sense of impending doom is manifest in the anxious faces of these ordinary citizens of Shildon gathered at a protest meeting in May 1982. The future of Shildon Works was in jeopardy and its closure would be a great blow to the Shildon community.

A deputation to stop the closure of Shildon Works arrived at No. 10 Downing Street on 2 March 1983 and handed in a petition of protest at the plans, which would raise unemployment in this 'one-industry' town to over 50 per cent. Seen here from left to right are: Derek Foster, MP for Bishop Auckland, Alan Roberts, Sedgefield Council's Chief Executive and its leading councillors, Wilf Edwards, Chairman, Bill Smith, Sam Carmedy and Warren McCourt. The visit was not a success and the historic Shildon Works closed in 1984 after 151 years, putting 1,200 people out of work.

CHAPTER SIX

The North Road Shops, Darlington

In October 1857, having outgrown the capacity of Shildon Works, the S&DR decided to build a new locomotive works. This is the first locomotive to be constructed at the North Road Shops, being contractor-built in 1864. William Bouch, who had succeeded Timothy Hackworth at Shildon, chose North Road, Darlington. The workshops were opened on 1 January 1863 and covered an area of about 6 acres with a further 27 acres of land purchased for extensions. Prior to the building of the North Road Shops all repairs to Stockton & Darlington engines were done at Shildon. Within a few months the Company amalgamated with the North Eastern Railway, but it was not until 1877 that S&DR designs ceased to be built and NER locomotives were introduced. The North Road Shops were located on North Road, part of the former Edinburgh–London stage-coach route, within easy reach of North Road and Bank Top stations. William Bouch became the first Locomotive Superintendent and took charge of the North Road Shops at a salary of £450 per annum. He held the post until 1875, a longer tenure than any of those who followed him.

A general view of the North Road Shops, Darlington, October 1964. The works were specially designed to allow for considerable expansion and centralization of repair work on the S&DR. In 1867 a new storehouse was built, and in 1873 a new blacksmiths' shop, brass foundry, coppersmiths' shop and joiners' shop were erected. In 1876 a new boiler shop was added, and in 1884 a new forge and two new erecting shops were put up. In 1898 new stores offices, mess rooms and extensions to the brass foundry were constructed. In 1903 a new erecting shop was built and in 1911 a new paint shop and boiler and tender shop were erected at Stooperdale to relieve the congestion at the North Road Shops.

The boys at the back of the group, photographed at the North Road Shops, Darlington, just before the outbreak of the First World War, are fourteen years old and in their first job. There was no shortage of work at that time. The number of men and boys employed when the North Road Shops were first opened in 1863 was about 150, and the wages totalled about £143 per week. In July 1914 2,396 people were employed there and the wage bill came to £4,480 per week. This was an average of 37*s* 6*d* per week in 1914 compared with 19*s* per week in 1863. During this period shop hours were reduced from 59 to 53 per week.

A Kendall and Gent profiling and channelling milling machine in the machine shop, North Road Shops, 1953. It is being used to profile-mill four locomotive coupling rods simultaneously.

Part of the complex array of machines at the North Road Shops, 1964.

A new engine being made at the North Road Shops, 16 July 1954. Many LNER high-capacity steam locomotives, including the Class V2 and A1, were built at the North Road Shops. After nationalization BR Standard locomotives were also built there.

Class A2, No. 60530, 4–6–2, *Sayajirao* being overhauled at the North Road Shops, 29 September 1964. It is named after the famous racehorse that won the 1947 St Leger. It was built in March 1948 at Doncaster and ended its days pulling 3 hour expresses between Glasgow and Aberdeen. It was the last but one of its class in service and was withdrawn in November 1966.

During 1914 a ten-strong fleet of 0–4+4–0, 1500 volts, DC electric locomotives were built at the North Road Shops, Darlington. As part of a new development on the Yorkshire bank of the Tees downstream of Port Clarence, later to become Middlesbrough, an extension of the S&DR from riverside wharves at Bowesfield Lane, Stockton, later to become Bowesfield Junction, was opened on 27 December 1830. In 1913 the Shildon–Newport, Middlesbrough, route was chosen for a pilot scheme for railway electrification. Work started on this infrastructure on 16 June 1913. In about 1915 electrical locomotive No. 3, the first electric goods engine, was making trial runs along the Shildon–Newport route. Here it is seen alongside an NER, Class 2, 0–6–0 goods engine. The years of the Depression during the 1920s and 1930s had a detrimental effect on railway freight and in 1935 electrification, no longer a commercially viable proposition, was abandoned.

Electric locomotive No. 13, 4–6–4, was Sir Vincent Raven's (Chief Mechanical Engineer of the NER) main-line electric-express passenger locomotive. It was ordered from the North Road Shops, Darlington, on 26 January 1921 and was out-shopped in May 1922. Apart from various trials and demonstration runs on the Shildon–Newport section, it never did any real work. On Sunday 4 June 1922 it hauled a test train from Newport to Shildon composed of seventeen coaches and a dynamometer car, a total weight of 460 tons. It maintained an average speed of 42mph and is best remembered for that. Apart from being seen at occasional exhibitions during the early 1930s, No. 13 languished at the Darlington (Stooperdale) paint shops. It was sold for scrap on 15 December 1950.

A general view of the North Road Shops with work in progress, 1930s. As early as October 1864, when the first locomotive was built there, the NER had already standardized its tenders as six-wheeled vehicles. With the exception of only one batch in 1949, all subsequent building was of six-wheeled tenders. Because tenders were simply carriers of coal and water, few technical improvements were required. However, the North Road Shops did introduce some interesting features. Tenders fitted to the long boiler engines had a total weight in working order of 22 tons 2cwt and carried 4 tons of coal and 1,600 gallons of water. Empty they weighed 11 tons. By 1913 the North Road Shops were putting the same coal and 25 per cent more water capacity into their tank engines. In 1948 they turned out the first batch of twenty-three tenders with capacities of 9 tons of coal and 5,000 gallons of water. These weighed 29cwt when empty and 60 tons 7cwt in working order. Thus, despite an increase of almost three times in the total weight, the ratio of weight carried to empty weight remained fairly constant.

The first Type 2, 1,160hp locomotive D5094, which was also the first main-line diesel-electric to be built at the North Road Shops, is on show, January 1960. The first batch of diesel-electrics comprised twenty diesels, all of which were completed by August 1964. Early in 1961 the centre bay of the main erecting shop was walled off to form a separate enclosure for main-line diesel-electric locomotive repairs, while the engine gear shop on the north side of the erecting shop became a diesel rail car and transmission repair shop. The new Engine Shop was converted completely to diesel locomotion construction after the last steam engine was built in June 1957. The adjacent shop catered for electrical repairs to diesel locomotives.

In October 1957, ninety-three years after the first locomotive was built at the North Road Shops, No. 84029, 2–6–2, became the last steam locomotive to be built there.

A J26 class steam engine being demolished in Darlington's scrap depot in 1960 when the North Road Shops were facing the same fate. It was designed in 1898.

The new engine shops at the North Road Shops, seen here in 1962, now turned over completely to diesel locomotion construction. Diesel-electric shunting engines were first built there in 1952. In 1954 BR introduced its Modernization and Re-equipment Plan and that year the staff at the North Road Shops, which in 1948 had numbered 3,548, increased to 3,815. Locomotive output was forty-nine new engines per annum, including sixteen diesel-electric shunting locomotives. That year 481 general, 48 intermediate classified and 230 non-classified repairs were carried out.

The three bays that formed the western entrances to the main erection shops, 24 September 1962. The steaming shed is on the left and the tyre park is on the right.

This fine view of the western end of the main erection shop includes, left to right, two 350hp shunters, two J-94 pilots, an English Electric Type 4 and a B1 locomotive, 1964.

The North Road Shops were first earmarked for closure by Beeching in 1962, but managed to win a stay of execution. At that time there were 648 skilled, 380 semi-skilled, 128 unskilled and 76 junior workers on the shop floor, a total staff of 1,232. All were apprehensive because they realized that events were stacked against them. Mr Tom Hodgson, a semi-skilled machinist grade one and an NUR member, seen here in 1965, said, 'I've worked here 30 years and I'm wondering who will take me on. I'm looking round for a job already. The younger men lack the experience we have and industry needs a balance of young and old. I would like to stay on this type of work but I've done other and I'd be happy to change again for the chance of a job.' He was a man of whom a management representative said, 'In all the times I have been in this shop I have never seen him away from his machine.'

Mr Bob Robson was a fitter-erector, aged forty-five in 1962, with four children still at home, three of whom worked. He was a skilled man and an AEU member. He said, 'I was bitter about the closure. I've felt bitter all along. We are as economic a shop as any other.' Notices had gone up in the North Road Shops that between 60 and 70 fitters and between 30 and 40 electricians were needed in Doncaster. This had annoyed the men who reasoned that if the men were in Darlington why could the work scheduled for Doncaster not be carried out in Darlington? Sadly, the problem was greater than that and it all boiled down to overheads and running costs.

NOTICE

IN CONSULTATION WITH THE TRADE UNIONS IT HAS BEEN DECIDED THAT THE FUTURE PLANNING SHOULD BE MADE KNOWN IN THOSE WORKS WHICH WILL CONTINUE AND THOSE WORKS WHICH ARE SCHEDULED FOR CLOSURE. SO FAR AS DARLINGTON NORTH ROAD AND STOOPERDALE ARE CONCERNED, A DECISION HAS BEEN TAKEN THAT THESE WORKS WILL CONTINUE UNTIL 1965 AND THEREAFTER BE CLOSED.

SPECIAL MEASURES WILL BE TAKEN TO REDUCE HARDSHIP CREATED BY REDUNDANCY AND THE UNDER-NOTED ARE THE TERMS WHICH HAVE BEEN IMPROVED AS A RESULT OF REPRESENTATION BY THE TRADE UNIONS, AND THESE ARE BEING FURTHER CONSIDERED BY THEM.

NOT LESS THAN SIX MONTHS NOTICE WILL BE GIVEN BEFORE THE FIRST DISCHARGES NECESSARY FOR CLOSURE START TO OPERATE. TO HELP OLDER MEN, AND MEN IN DIFFICULT EMPLOYMENT AREAS, LONGER NOTICE THAN SIX WEEKS TO BE GIVEN WHENEVER POSSIBLE. TO SUCH CASES RESETTLEMENT LUMP SUM PAYMENTS TO BE PAID TO MEN WISHING TO LEAVE UP TO THE FOLLOWING MAXIMUM PERIODS PRIOR TO NORMAL DISCHARGE DATES:—

PERIOD

AGE ON LEAVING RAILWAY SERVICE. 1	GENERAL RULE AT ALL WORKS OTHER THAN THOSE IN COL. III 2	MEN EMPLOYED AT GLASGOW, DARLINGTON, WALKER GATE, EARLESTOWN & HORWICH WORKS. III
UP TO 40 YEARS	6 WEEKS	10 WEEKS
40 TO 50	8 WEEKS	12 WEEKS
50 TO UNDER 55	10 WEEKS	14 WEEKS
55 AND OVER	12 WEEKS	AT ANY TIME AFTER NOTICE OF CLOSURE OF THEIR WORKS HAS BEEN ANNOUNCED.

IN ADDITION TO THESE MEASURES SPECIAL FACILITIES IN VARIOUS WAYS ARE BEING GIVEN TO HELP MEN TO OBTAIN OTHER EMPLOYMENT, AND DETAILS CAN BE GIVEN ON REQUEST.

The writing is on the wall, September 1965. The notice explaining the closure of the North Road and Stooperdale works with details of the redundancy procedures.

In 1962 British Rail Workshops Division was created with centralized control and a policy of rationalizing main works. Many workshops, including the North Road Shops, were to be closed because of a considerable reduction in the overall workload. That same year the North Road Shops was being televised, as seen here, for the television programme *Tonight*.

On 4 September 1962 employees at the North Road Shops organized a protest march to draw attention to their deteriorating work prospects. It was a very worrying time for the workforce, but even at that late hour a glimmer of hope remained that the shops would be saved. As this picture of crowded High Row, Darlington, shows, most of the faces are etched with concern about their future.

At a meeting with a British Railways Board official held in London on 14 January 1964 it was made clear to a delegation from Darlington that there was no hope of delaying the closure of the North Road Shops. The delegation was led by Mr A.T. Bourne-Arton, Conservative MP for Darlington, and Labour Councillor Cecil Spence. They spent 1 hour and 45 minutes discussing the works' problems with Mr H.O. Houchen, General Manager of the British Railways Board Workshops Division. After the meeting Mr Bourne-Arton said, 'We were very well received, as we always are, and we got a sympathetic hearing. But it was made quite clear that there was no hope of modifying the plan for the closure rundown.' Councillor Spence, Chairman of Darlington Development Committee, refused to talk in detail about the meeting on his return to Darlington, merely commenting, 'I am sickened by the whole business. They had obviously made up their minds before they saw us. I have nothing else to say.'

'There's only me left. All the machinery has been dismantled. All the men who looked after me have gone. There's not even a saucer of milk. Life can be tough for a redundant loco works mouser miaow!'

Workers at the North Road Shops finished for the day, 20 September 1962.

The North Road Shops finished for good. It closed in 1966 with a reduced staff of 2,759, ending more than a century of locomotive building and repairing on the site.

CHAPTER SEVEN

Railway Mania, 1836–58

The first passenger train drawn by a steam engine did not begin its journey to Stockton from Witton Park and Etherley Collieries, at the western end of the S&DR, because Etherley and Brusselton inclines were in the way and no locomotive could tackle those – fixed engines and ropes were the only way to overcome these natural features of the landscape. It was from the eastern foot of Brusselton incline, near the Masons Arms, that *Locomotion No. 1* began its epic journey on 27 September, 1825. Eleven years later the newly born railway age had evolved into a lusty enterprise that was quickly developing into railway mania.

Not all Timothy Hackworth's locomotives were built for the S&DR. *Braddyll* was one of four built for the South Hetton Colliery. Its life as a locomotive ended in 1875, although it continued for many more years as a snow plough.

Darlington North Road Station, *c.* 1900. In 1842 North Road station replaced the small goods warehouse that had been converted into a booking office, waiting room and cottage, along with a narrow wooden platform, which had sufficed as Darlington's station from 1833. The station is west of North Road, not actually on it.

These people are investigating an old story about North Road station. By 1850 the station cottage had been demolished and a coal cellar had been built on the site. One winter's night in 1850 James Durham, a night watchman, was on duty at North Road station. Having completed an inspection and feeling cold and hungry, he went down some steps to the porter's cellar where there was a fire and a gas light. The coal cellar was adjacent to the porter's room. Durham sat on a bench facing the fire and was about to eat when a strange man, followed by a large black retriever, entered from the coal cellar. The man wore a smart cutaway coat with gilt buttons and a stand-up collar. The two men stared at each other. Then, his eyes still on Durham, the stranger moved in front of the fireplace. He watched Durham with a curious smile on his face, then struck him. Durham struck back and 'my hand passed through him and skinned the knuckles on the fireplace'. The man fell back towards the fire and the dog attacked Durham, hurting his leg but leaving no bite marks. The stranger recovered, clicked his tongue at the dog and returned to the coal cellar. Durham lit his lantern and followed. There was no way out, but there was no sign of either man or dog. The story was checked. What Durham did not know was that a railway man called Winter, owner of a black dog, shot himself in the vicinity. He had been dressed as Durham had seen him and his body had lain undetected in the cellar for some time.

25
W. KITCHING MAKER DARLINGTON
DERWENT

Derwent, a 'Tory' class locomotive, 0–6–0, was built for the S&DR Co. by A. Kitching, founder of Whessoe Ltd, Darlington, and was subsequently purchased by Messrs Pease for use on their private lines. It was presented to the NER by Messrs Pease and Partners in March 1898.

TO THE DIRECTORS

OF THE

STOCKTON AND DARLINGTON RAILWAY COMPANY.

GENTLEMEN,

THE Half-yearly Accounts to June 30th, 1854, are presented herewith, and I beg to invite your attention to the annexed abstracts and calculations, giving a comparison of quantities and amounts at various periods.

The state of the Loan Account will be seen from the following table :—

	3¼ ℘ Cent.	3½ ℘ Cent.	3¾ ℘ Cent.	4 ℘ Cent.	4¼ ℘ Cent.	4½ ℘ Cent.	4¾ ℘ Cent.	5 ℘ Cent.	Total.
	£	£	£	£	£	£	£	£	£
December 31, 1853.	300	113,196	5,900	261,052	400	109,573	500	63,144	554,065
June 30, 1854	300	33,910	5,900	297,364	3,500	113,072	500	64,465	519,012

After deducting the available assets from the £519,012, the net amount stands £476,401 17s. 6d., as shown in the Half-yearly Accounts.

The quantities of various kinds of Traffic passing upon the Line in the **year 1849** and the **year 1853,** have been as under :—

	1849.	1853.
	Tons	Tons.
Coal and Coke Exported	414,966	329,663
,, Landsale and Manufactures	426,267	611,100
,, York Junction	342,165	528,909
Cleveland Ironstone	Nil.	372,346
Weardale do.	144,187	57,210
Limestone	81,012	92,315
Lime	37,106	39,535
Building Stones, &c.	38,927	59,025
Merchandise	166,220	256,738
	1,650,850	2,346,841
	Numbers.	Numbers.
Passengers	369,123	426,764

The quantities sent on to the Line in the **half-year** ending June 30th, 1849, and the **half-year** ending June 30th, 1854, stand thus :—

	Half-year ending June 30, 1849.	Half-year ending June 30, 1854.
	Tons.	Tons.
Coal and Coke	530,490	757,146
Ironstone	73,660	212,985
Lime	16,431	17,673
Limestone	24,410	36,565
Building Stones, &c.	26,633	88,224
Merchandise	91,683	179,499
	763,307	1,292,092
	Numbers.	Number.
Passengers	170,438	230,771

ARCHIVE TEACHING UNIT: THE STOCKTON AND DARLINGTON RAILWAY 1825 33

The half-yearly accounts for the S&DR to 30 June 1854. The figures are healthy and show substantial increases in mineral traffic, merchandise and passenger traffic when compared with the half year ending 30 June 1849.

The revenue of the S&DR for 1827, its second financial year, exceeded estimates made prior to the opening of the line by about £2,000. It was sufficient to satisfy the proprietors, yet it came to only £18,404 4*s* 4*d*. The rapid increase of trade and revenue that was to follow caught everyone by surprise. By 1850 revenue had amounted to only £169,690 but by 1860 it had leaped to £389,352, an unprecedented increase. Preference shares, like this one dated 1858, sold very quickly. In 1863 the S&DR ceased to be an independent company and its traffic and revenue returns merged with those of the NER. That year the total revenue of the company was £496,690, and in 1867, the last year for which the figures relating to the Darlington section have been extracted, it had risen to £758,815, very nearly double what it was in 1860.

THE

Stockton & Darlington Railway Company.

CLASS A PREFERENTIAL 5 PER CENT SHARES.

Nº 15415 £25

ACT OF 1858

This is to Certify that Edward Gedman Kirkpatrick of Barham Court, in the County of Kent, Merchant; Lunn Saul, of Brunswick, Cumberland, and Charles John Rennell, of No. 2, Eaton Place, Middlesex, Esquire, are the Proprietors of the CLASS A PREFERENTIAL SHARE Numbered 15415 in the STOCKTON & DARLINGTON RAILWAY COMPANY, subject to the Rules, Regulations and Orders of the said Company.

Given under the Common Seal of the said Company. Dated the Twenty Fourth day of September in the year of our Lord one thousand eight hundred & fifty eight.

Thos. MacNay Secretary

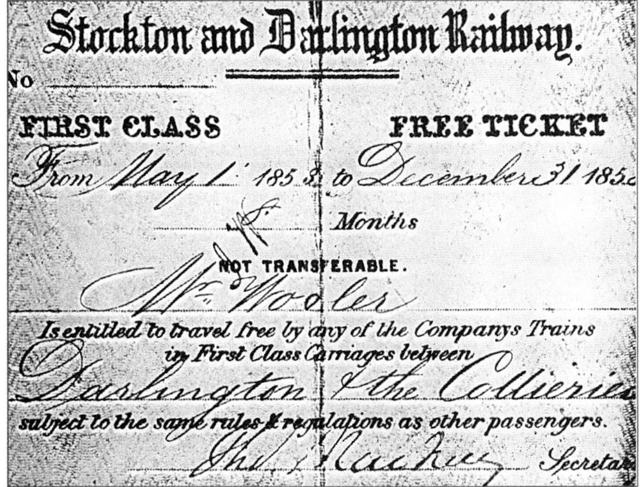

Stockton and Darlington Railway.

No

FIRST CLASS FREE TICKET

From May 1st 1853 to December 31 1853

Months

NOT TRANSFERABLE.

Mr. Wooler

Is entitled to travel free by any of the Companys Trains in First Class Carriages between Darlington & the Collieries subject to the same rules & regulations as other passengers.

Thos. MacNay Secretary

Not everyone was obliged to purchase a ticket. Some privileged passengers were entitled to travel free, first class, by any of the Company's trains between Darlington and the collieries. Railway officials were the usual recipients of free tickets.

The railway children: Miles Clifton, David Holiday and Tony Broomhead at Shildon before being given a ride in a locomotive, 21 July 1993. 'What would you like to be when you grow up, boys?' 'Please sir, we'd all like to be engine drivers.'

Locomotion No. 1 is shown on one of a set of commemorative stamps issued by the Post Office in 1975 to mark the development of railways through the steam era to the less-romantic but much more expensive high-speed age.

This painting of *Locomotion No. 1* is at the Railway Institute, North Road, Darlington. This Eponymous class, 0–4–0, locomotive, designed and built by Robert Stephenson and Co. and delivered in September 1825 in time for the official opening of the line and now preserved, is synonymous with the S&DR. When, in 1863, the S&DR was absorbed by the NER, two of those most involved with *Locomotion No. 1*, George Stephenson and Edward Pease, were quite rightly venerated. But the man who contributed so much to the success of both men was ignored. Thankfully, the history of this gifted and upright man, Timothy Hackworth, is now well known.

CHAPTER EIGHT

The UK's Most Complete Monopoly

The emblem of the NER. The development of the railway network in the North East between 1854 and 1866 was strongly influenced by two major developments. The first of these was the struggle for the Cleveland ironstone district. It was a period of intense rivalry between the most important companies in the region and was brought about by the discovery of commercially viable iron ore deposits near Middlesbrough in about 1850. The second factor was the series of attempted invasions of the North East by outside companies intent on gaining a share of regional traffic. This period of competition was particularly fierce between 1857 and 1866. It led to a realignment of relationships between hitherto rival local companies and eventually to the almost complete elimination of railway competition in the district. In 1862 the Newcastle & Carlisle became part of the NER, followed, in 1863, by the S&DR, and in 1865 by the West Hartlepool and a number of smaller railways. By 1866 every line between the Humber and the Tyne was tied in one form or another to the NER, which was acknowledged to be 'the most complete monopoly in the United Kingdom'.

The comparison between 'Experiment' and this railway carriage, which was in use at about the time the North Eastern Railway incorporated the S&DR, clearly shows the advances in railway carriage design over forty years. 'Experiment' was the very first passenger coach, and its name and the Company's motto '*Periculum privatum utilitas publica*' were painted on its sides. It was used at the opening of the S&DR and began a regular service on 10 October 1825. Later it was leased to one Thomas Close at 2 guineas a week. The Company safeguarded its interests through an agreement with a clause that stated that 'the first time he is seen intoxicated he will be dismissed and the sum due to him in wages shall be forfeited'. This horse-drawn coach, which had no springs of any kind, ran from Stockton to Darlington and back daily except Sundays.

In 1833 the S&DR superseded horses with steam locomotives. In 1844 an act of Parliament forced all the railway companies to put roofs over third-class coaches. However, there was always a tendency for the various railway companies to do nothing until they were pressurized by public opinion or some tragic accident forced the issue. Coach development, therefore, was slow but logical. The short four-wheeled vehicle seen here was followed by the longer, more stable and more comfortable six-wheeler.

The excesses of railway promotional activity were most apparent between 1854 and 1866. This competitive expansion of the whole railway network was finally halted when a general commercial crisis began to develop in about 1866. Although the NER continued its expansion from 1,278 route miles in 1870 to 1,730 in 1913, this was almost completely in response to the needs of trade and industry as distinct from the competitive and highly speculative promotions of previous years. It was during the years between 1866 and 1914 that the NER settled down to capitalize on the efforts of an earlier age. Near the beginning of this period of consolidation, in 1875, a railway jubilee was held at Darlington to celebrate the fiftieth anniversary of the opening of the S&DR. This sketch of the exhibition of locomotives was featured in the supplement to the *Illustrated London News* of 9 October 1875.

The unveiling of Joseph Pease's statue at the north end of High Row, 28 September 1875. This was the highlight of Darlington's celebrations to commemorate the fiftieth anniversary of the opening of the S&DR. It was erected in recognition of his extraordinary ability and his tremendous efforts to boost the town's economy. The man with his hand on the barrier is His Grace the 4th Duke of Cleveland who did the honours.

The fiftieth anniversary celebrations in full swing, 27 September 1875. A procession of people marching behind their respective banners and preceded by S&DR dignitaries wends its way along Tubwell Row, bedecked with bunting and packed with revellers. Never had Darlington seen such crowds.

Mrs Doris Cook of Malton proudly displays a special dinner plate, 28 August 1975. It is inscribed 'Railway Jubilee Commemoration, held in Darlington. September 27th, 1875.' It had lain in a drawer, forgotten until a *Northern Echo* railway colour supplement reminded her that she had a treasure in the attic.

Mr Eddie Marsh of Middleton-in-Teesdale inspects some commemorative sheet music, August 1975. William Crawford, station master at Bishop Auckland, celebrated the S&DR's fiftieth anniversary in style by composing 'The Jubilee Waltzes 1875'.

North Eastern, No. 910, 0–6–0 was built at Gateshead in 1875. It was the only locomotive to take part in the S&DR cavalcades of 1875, 1925 and 1975.

George Stephenson would not recognize the housing estate, top left, but he would have no problem with Shildon tunnel and the approach cutting. They connect the Bishop Auckland & Weardale Railway at South Church with the S&DR at Shildon. The tunnel was built without Parliament's blessing, opened on 19 April 1842 and sold to the Wear Valley Railway on 22 July 1847. The single line, seen here in 1979, was originally double. The line is still in use.

Shildon Station, August 1975. Daniel Adamson served his apprenticeship under Timothy Hackworth and became one of the great engineers of his day. It was from Daniel Adamson's coach house that the first coaches to haul passengers from New Shildon along the S&DR set off. In railway terms passengers were always 'hauled' and coals were 'led'. Later the Mason's Arms became New Shildon's starting point and remained so until 1842 when Shildon's first railway station was built. The platform was partly constructed of old sandstone blocks, originally used as sleepers when the S&DR was first built, and had the dubious distinction of being the dreariest railway station in the UK. The sleepers were removed recently when Shildon station was refurbished.

Heighington is one of the oldest stations along the S&DR. The part of the station seen here is twinned with a place in France called 'Hommes'.

An unnamed North Road Works 2–2–2, W. Bouch-designed locomotive being 'sparked up' for the 1925 cavalcade of steam. It came into service in 1869 and was withdrawn in 1908.

In 1885 the NER produced a 2–4–0 express passenger class of twenty locomotives, all of which survived to become LNER class E5. Nominally designed by a committee chaired by NER General Manager Henry Tennant, the class was usually referred to as 'Tennant' and the first of the class built at North Road, No. 1463, took part in the procession as exhibit number twenty in the 1925 cavalcade. On withdrawal from service in 1927, No. 1463 was restored and is now located at Darlington North Road Railway Museum.

The date plate from locomotive No. 1463.

NER Locomotive No. 1310 is typical of several built for the NER at the end of the twentieth century. It was constructed in 1891. The locomotive was rescued from the National Coal Board in 1965 and carefully restored, most of the work being carried out by a Stockton man, Mr K. Cockerill.

This immaculate J21 class locomotive, 0–6–0 on its 100th birthday, 25 May 1989. Joining in the celebrations are, left to right: Gary Bunt, Christopher Hallam, Colin Nicholson and David Telford.

Bank Top station, 2 April 1993. The original station at Bank Top, Darlington, was an untidy wooden shed. Queen Victoria was not amused at its shabby appearance when she visited Darlington on 28 May 1849. She pointed out that for the main-line station of the very place in which the railway had been born to look so down at heel was just not good enough. The Great North of England Railway, whose station it was, did make some improvements, but it was thirty-eight years before Bank Top station was built at a cost of £110,000, in 1887.

At the eastern end of the line Stockton station, seen here on 16 September 1978, was equally grand and almost as empty as Darlington Bank Top.

With the S&DR now part of the NER, and Bank Top station, Darlington, now operative, long-distance travel in expresses like the 'Flying Scotsman', seen here in 1888, became a reality. This locomotive is 'Stirling Single', No. 53, 4–2–2, designed by Patrick Stirling, which was considered by many to be the most graceful locomotive ever built. The sweeping curves of the smokebox flow smoothly around the cylinders, and the top of the boiler does not have the customary steam dome. Known as 'eight footers' because of the diameter of their driving wheels, the later locomotives were 50 per cent more powerful than the prototype and pulled the principal East Coast expresses until after the end of the nineteenth century. Stirlings like the *Flying Scotsman* took part in races to the North in 1888 and 1895.

The opulent interior of a Great Northern dining car, pulled by the *Flying Scotsman*, *c.* 1900. The 'Flying Scotsman' symbolized East Coast express passenger motive power with locomotives like the *Flying Scotsman*, *Henry Oakley* and *Sir Nigel Gresley*.

Progress is seldom made without cost. On 15 November 1910 there was a collision at Bank Top, Darlington, which toppled an engine and a tender unit, as this photograph records.

Sadly, despite stringent safety measures, occasional accidents happened on the S&DR. This collision at Darlington station occurred on 9 March 1929 and resulted in the deaths of two people.

CHAPTER NINE

The LNER Takes Over

The railway centenary service at Bank Top station, 1925. The S&DR was absorbed by the NER on 13 July 1863, and Timothy Hackworth, who also had his own business at Soho Works, Shildon, was appointed foreman of the line. By 1914 its gross income had almost trebled. The NER had grown substantially to meet the rising long-term demand for its services, but over that period expenditure rose more rapidly than income and the return on capital fell. On 1 January 1923 the NER became part of the new LNER, formed as a result of the Railways Act of 1921, by which Parliament decreed that 120 independent railway companies should merge into groups. The LNER was the largest and by far the strongest constituent of the group because of volume of freight and mineral traffic generated in its industrial area and the steady west–east flow of coal from the mines to the east-coast ports for shipment. The Company was proud of its lineage that stemmed from the beginning of the railway age when the opening of the S&DR in 1825 heralded the beginning of the public, as distinct from the private, railway company operated by steam locomotives.

Heighington station seen here in about 1900, but looking much as it did during the First World War. Wayside stations have always been an important part of village life. They were a source of useful information and a meeting place for regular passengers, long-distance passengers, day trippers, locals on shopping trips, schoolchildren and farmers, often entraining cattle. They also acted as recruiting grounds for the railway service. It was an accepted fact and a source of pride among railway personnel that passengers and other customers should be helped to the best of the railwayman's ability and that every effort should be made to run the trains punctually.

A hat made for E.T. Barrell, Chief of Police, North Eastern Area, and worn at the 1925 centenary celebrations of the S&DR. Its container was made for the London and North Eastern Railway. Within a short time of the creation of the big four railways, the 'and' was removed and the initials contracted to LNER, as London Midland and Scottish was shortened to LMS. Both sets of initials were much easier to say without the 'and', and their enclosure in a lozenge produced a 'totem' that was to become very widely used and recognized.

When just over 2½ years from the inception of the LNER, the 100th anniversary of the opening of the S&DR took place, it came at a time of diminishing passenger journeys and a huge drop in annual tonnage carried by the LNER. At a centenary banquet held in the LNER's Faverdale Works, Darlington, on 2 July 1925, Sir Arthur Pease called for sacrifice from both workers and management to regain Britain's world trade. He urged road and rail to co-operate, it being a great mistake for both rail and road to lose money by both trying to compete for the same traffic. Viscount Grey of Falloden, an LNER director who presided at the banquet, stated that there was a feeling not so much of congratulation about the past as anxiety about the future as railways were passing through a difficult time and were unable to undertake as many developments as they would like. The guests of honour, the Duke and Duchess of York, later King George VI and Queen Elizabeth, inspect early railway stock at Faverdale during the centenary celebrations.

The Duchess of York inspecting a guard of honour outside Stockton station during the S&DR centenary celebrations, in July 1925.

The Duchess of York, escorted by Viscount Grey of Falloden, inspects some early locomotives. Although the centenary was 27 September 1925, it was celebrated in July because a meeting of the International Railway Congress was also taking place at this time. On Wednesday 1 July the Royal Train steamed into Darlington's Bank Top station 3 minutes early and the Earl of Durham welcomed the Duke and Duchess of York. Crowds waved and cheered as the royal visitors travelled by car through flag-decked streets to Faverdale Wagon Works where more spectators stood at the gates 'waiting on the tip-toes of expectancy', as John North, columnist of the *Northern Echo* wrote.

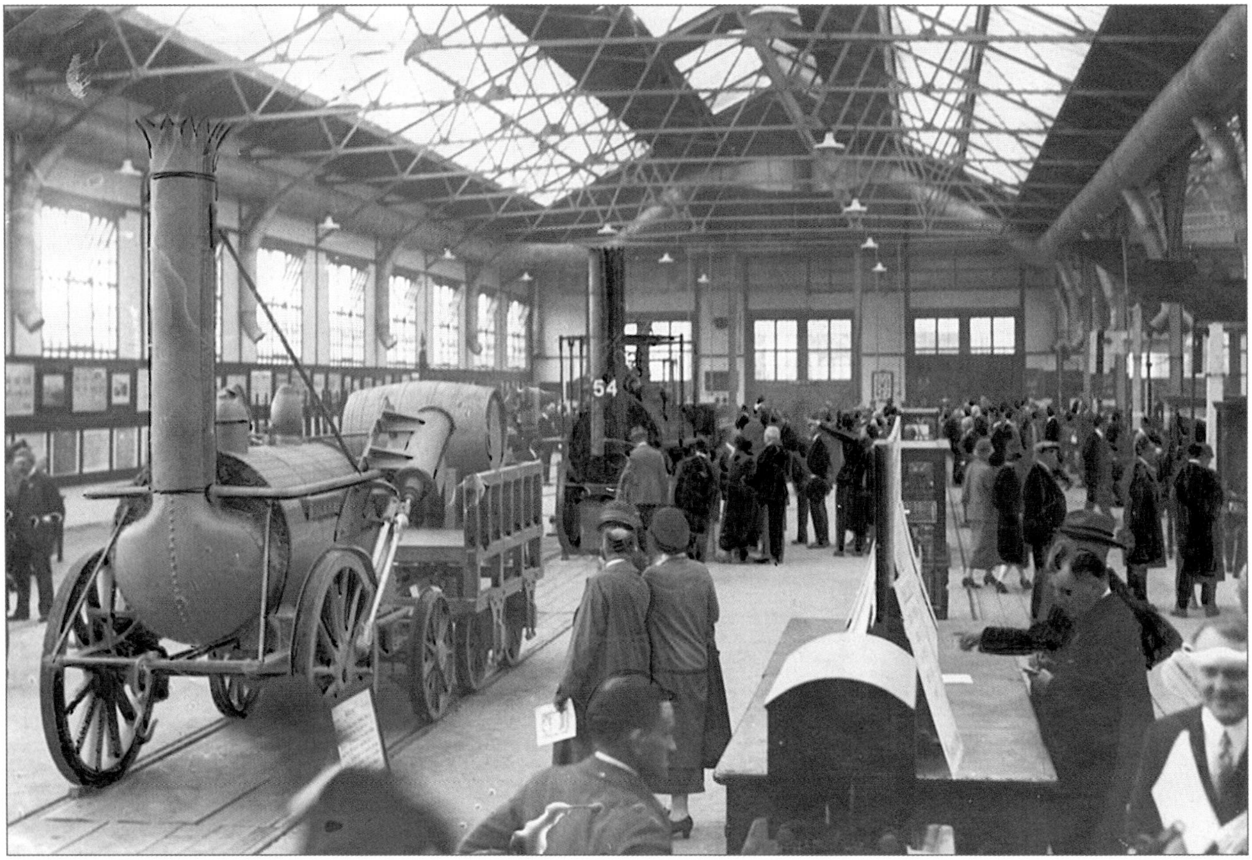

A general view of delegates at the International Railway Congress Exhibition, Faverdale Wagon Works, 1 July 1925. The next day the Duke and Duchess of York travelled by train to Urlay Nook, between Stockton and Darlington, to take seats in a grandstand to watch a parade of fifty-three locomotives and trains described in LNER publicity as 'a unique and historic occasion which cannot recur'. A quarter of a million people attended.

At 9.45 a.m. on 2 July 1925 a 6 mile long procession began to leave the Billingham Beck Branch at North Shore Junction. The first exhibit in the event was George Stephenson's Hetton Colliery locomotive, built in 1822, and seen here. By the time it led the 1925 steam procession marking the 100th anniversary of public railways it had undergone many rebuilds. The man at the controls, not seen here, was driver Suddes.

Derwent, seen here being removed from Darlington Bank Top station before being transported to the new North Road Museum, 1975. It was number two in the procession and was driven by George Danby of Shildon. A typical Hackworth-type goods locomotive, *Derwent* was built by W. and A. Kitchin of Darlington in 1845 and after several years of service on the S&DR, it was sold in 1869 to Pease and Partners for use on colliery lines.

No. 1275 was built in 1874 by Dubs and Co. of Glasgow for use on the Stockton and Darlington section of the NER. The last survivor of the 'long boiler' type 0–6–0, No. 1275 was withdrawn from Malton Shed in 1923 and carefully restored and repainted. After spending several years in York Railway Museum, No. 1275 went on loan to Darlington North Road Railway Museum in 1975.

In 1863 the pioneering S&DR was absorbed by the North Eastern Railway and twenty-two years later this company produced a class of twenty 2–4–0 'Tennants', all of which survived to become LNER class E5 locomotives. One of these locomotives, seen here, took part in the hundredth anniversary celebration of the opening of the S&DR.

On 13 December 1929 Darlington-built LNER locomotive 10,000, *Hush Hush*, 4–6–4, had its first main-line run. It is seen here at Durham station, 1935. It did yeoman service hauling express passenger trains between Kings Cross and Newcastle. The LNER had a life span of only twenty-five years, from 1923 until 1948, a dramatic period in the history of the United Kingdom. Its southern area comprised three 'Greats', Great Northern, Great Eastern and Great Central. North of this area was the territory of the NER, a well-managed, prosperous line with a proud lineage stretching back to the S&DR at the very genesis of railways. The LNER had lots of ideas but was strapped for cash. Its directors hoped that the NER section would be able to support the weaker areas financially. These hopes faded away with depression in coal mining, iron and steel and ship-building. As far as net revenue was concerned the LNER's first year was its best. In 1926 revenue fell because of strikes and this fall became more rapid in the Depression years to 1932. Helped by re-armament, there was a gradual turn around in fortunes, which lasted until 1938, a year of severe setbacks with revenue down and expenditure up. A recovery was staged in 1939 but it represented a change from peace to war.

On 28 September 1935 the LNER celebrated the 110th birthday of its ancestor the S&DR, by introducing to the travelling public the 'Silver Jubilee', the first train running on a British railway to be streamlined throughout. It was drawn by a class A4 locomotive, 4–6–2, No. 2509, the *Silver Link*. The train was designed to run at exceptionally high speeds while giving the travelling public a special degree of comfort. The locomotive's name came from the *Lay of the Last Minstrel*, Sir Walter Scott's second major work, published in 1805. 'True love's the gift which God has given to man alone beneath heaven. It is the secret sympathy, the *silver link*, which heart to heart and mind to mind, in body and in soul can bind.'

The original streamlining of the *Silver Link* had the coupling in the centre recessed and the buffers flush with the frontage. No allowance was made in the streamlining to accommodate anyone working on the coupling, and this led to a railwayman so doing being squashed to death. Had the buffers been standing proud, he would have had a small chance of avoiding injury. With flush buffers he stood no chance. *Silver Link*, seen here outside No. 5 depot at ICI Wilton, has had its streamlining modified with both coupling and buffers standing proud but hidden by the man on the left. Its name and number are clearly seen, yet the locomotive is actually A4 *Bittern*, a sister engine that has been cosmetically restored by NELPG the North Eastern Locomotion Preservation Group to represent the long-since scrapped *Silver Link*.

LNER, class A3, 4-6-4, locomotive No. 2750 *Papyrus* leaving Kings Cross with a full head of steam, 5 March 1935. There is a dynamometer car immediately behind the tender. Driven by H. Gutteridge, it had travelled non-stop from Kings Cross to Newcastle. On the return trip, driven by W. Sparshott, a speed of 105mph was reached on the descent of Stoke Bank, and a little further on 108mph was attained. *Papyrus* covered the distance between Newcastle and Kings Cross in 231 minutes 41 seconds, a feat that set the scene for the next Gresley 'Pacific' class A4.

This 'Coronation' streamlined express is moving out of York station on its first run north, 9 July 1937. 'Coronation' expresses were usually pulled by 'Dominion' class streamlined Pacifics.

LNER, 4–6–2, No. 4498, *Sir Nigel Gresley*, was built in 1937, the year Mr Gresley received a knighthood for his services to railways both as an engineer and as a locomotive designer. It was the 100th class A Pacific built to his design. It was intended that this engine would run non-stop trains between London and the northern cities on the LNER system. Together, locomotive and tender were 71 ft long and weighed about 167 tons. It was built for maximum efficiency when travelling at high speed, and it and others of its class were expected to travel some 75,000 miles between major overhauls. In the late 1950s *Sir Nigel Gresley* exceeded 110mph on a special train.

On 3 July 1936 class A4 locomotive, 4–6–2, No. 4468, *Mallard*, the greatest steam locomotive in the world, was driven at a speed of 125mph between Grantham and Peterborough, thus achieving a world record for steam traction that has never been broken. On 2 June 1962 the eight-coach 'Aberdeen Flyer' made an historic run between Kings Cross and Edinburgh, a distance of 392 miles. It was the longest non-stop journey ever by an excursion train in this country and *Mallard* hauled it. Here it is seen on 3 June 1998, back on the rails for the first time in twenty-three years and still going strong.

In 1936 five LNER class V2, 2–6–2, locomotives were built as forerunners of a new class designed to meet the ever-increasing demands of the day for fast and reliable mixed traffic locomotives. One of them, No. 4771, *Green Arrow*, seen here hauling 'The North Eastern', regularly hauled the 3.55 p.m. Scottish goods north from London. V2s made light work of main-line duties with rising traffic demands. At the outbreak of the Second World War almost 100 V2s were in service and in construction, which continued until 1944. The V2s could work easily as well as the larger Pacific locomotives, and LNER crews dubbed them 'the locomotives that won the war'. A total of 184 were built. V2s worked all the main routes of the LNER until the 1960s when new diesel-electric locomotives made them redundant. On withdrawal from service, *Green Arrow* was completely overhauled and repainted in the LNER livery of Apple Green, the engine's original colour.

CHAPTER TEN

Rail 150 Exhibition: Steam Cavalcade

During the Second World War, like all other railways, the LNER had to cope as best it could with heavy new demands and very few new resources. Following the war it had great plans for the future, including a £50 million programme of investment which was more than twice the company's total capital expenditure between 1923 and 1938. It had participated fully in the rethink about the role of the railways in the postwar world. It also approved a diesel-traction project for the whole of the East Coast Main Line services. But, with the election of a Labour government in 1945 with a strong overall majority, some form of nationalization was inevitable. Under nationalization LNER's investment programme was largely scrapped, as was its diesel-traction project. The LNER had led the world in fast, steam, locomotive-hauled trains, its personal relations were good and staff morale generally remained high despite frequent adverse situations. There was an inherent sense of pride in the LNER which was served by an enthusiastic staff and led by directors who knew how to run a railway. They devoted their lives to ensuring that the LNER lived up to its motto 'Forward' and that it led the way. With nationalization imminent, sixty-six senior LNER officers produced an illustrated, signed booklet setting out the railway's principal achievements between 1923 and 1947 and presented it to the LNER Directors. It was a fitting tribute to their management talent which was the greatest legacy of the LNER to British Railways.

Between 24 and 30 August 1975 a Rail 150 Exhibition was held to mark the 150th anniversary of the opening of the S&DR, the start of which is seen in this aerial photograph.

LNER 'Precedent' class, 2–4–0, No. 790 *Hardwicke*, introduced in 1873, leads the line-up at Shildon, 25 August 1975. In the summer of 1895, at a time of intense rivalry between the West Coast route (London & North Western Railway and Caledonian Railway) and the East Coast route (Great Northern Railway, North Eastern Railway and the North British Railway), *Hardwicke* raced the section from Crewe to Carlisle. Her finest performance was on 22 August 1895 when she covered 141 miles in 126 minutes. This included a climb over Shap summit at an average speed of 62.4mph. LMS 4–4–0 'Compound', No. 1000, behind *Hardwicke* was introduced in 1902. It was the first locomotive of Compound design. Compounds worked throughout the whole of the Midland system and in Scotland during the LMS days and some 240 of them were built.

LNER class D49, 4–4–0, No. 246 *Morayshire* is seen here at Shildon shed shunting LNER class V2, 2–6–2, No. 4771 *Green Arrow*, not much of which is seen. *Morayshire* was one of the seventy-six D49 class locomotives introduced in 1927, half of which were named after counties through which LNER traffic worked. The remainder were named after famous fox hunter packs, the class being known as 'Shires' or 'Hunts'.

This photograph links the Stockton & Darlington Railway's 100th, 150th and 175th celebrations. It was taken on 2 July 1925 and *Locomotion No. 1* was exhibit number fifty-four, the last one in the parade. As a *Northern Echo* reporter observed, it was 'the most brilliant spectacle of the whole wonderful parade'. *Locomotion No. 1* was the original, but its tender, ten chaldrons and the coach, the original of which was used by the S&DR committee on the opening day in 1825, were all replicas. They were filled with passengers in period costume and the 100-year-old, real *Locomotion No. 1* driven by a petrol engine concealed in the replica tender, belched out smoke made by burning waste. As it travelled towards Darlington, spectators spilled on to the line for a closer look, many placing coins on the rails to be flattened by the wheels of *Locomotion No. 1*. On approaching the grandstand at Darlington, a man carrying a red flag and riding a large, grey horse a safe distance in front of the train, as happened in 1825, rode on ahead of it. The train halted before the grandstand and bandsmen travelling in the two rear chaldrons struck up 'Auld Lang Syne'. The Duke and Duchess of York got to their feet and the assembled company bared their heads until the veteran engine moved away. A replica *Locomotion No. 1* led the 150th cavalcade very impressively.

As part of the opening ceremony LMS class 5 MT, 4–6–0, No. 4767 had the name *George Stephenson* conferred on it. Often described as the most successful locomotive built by the LMS, the class MTs were ideally suited to working on both freight and express-passenger duties. They were first introduced in 1934 and 842 were built. *George Stephenson* was number three in the cavalcade order.

The S&DR 150th anniversary cavalcade being marshalled at Shildon. The locomotive on the left is LMS class 5 MT, 4–6–0, No. 4767, *George Stephenson*. No. 2238, on the right, was introduced in 1918, one of Sir Vincent Raven's NER class T2, 0–8–0 locomotives, of which 120 were built between 1913 and 1918. No. 2238 was number four in the cavalcade.

BR class K1, 2–6–0 No. 2005 was number six in the cavalcade. The class K1, first introduced in 1949, was a simplified development of Sir Nigel Gresley's three-cylinder K4, which was specially built in 1937 for the arduous West Highland Line. K4s were all built by the North British Locomotive Co. Ltd in Glasgow between 1949 and 1950, No. 2005 being out-shopped in June 1949. No. 62005, as she became, spent all her working life in the North-East of England. In March 1965 she partnered the preserved K4, *The Great Marquess* on the last BR steam passenger train over the former Whitby–Pickering Railway, part of which has now been taken over by the North Yorkshire Moors Historical Railway Trust and is now a thriving tourist attraction. No. 62005 has the rare distinction among engines of having been used as a Royal engine when Her Majesty the Queen visited the North of England in both 1960 and 1967, the year the engines were withdrawn from service.

The 150th anniversary cavalcade viewed from the air, which puts the sheer scale of the undertaking into perspective.

Just the thing to bring out the crowds – the passing cavalcade, 150th anniversary, 1975. The leading engine is LSWR/SR class S15, 4–6–0, No. 841, *Green King*. The S15 class was introduced to the London & South Western Railway as a mixed-traffic version of Urie's express passenger 4–6–0 which later became 'King Arthur' class. The Southern Railway built more similar engines, the second batch of which differed in various ways from their earlier locomotives. No. 841 is one of the last batch and dates from 1936. Although designed primarily for parcels traffic, the locomotives were often used as passenger locomotives at peak holiday times.

This Scottish visitor, number seven in the cavalcade, is Caledonian Railway class 439, 0–4–4, No. 419, one of a class of ninety-one built between 1900 and 1925, a development of a locomotive to the 1884 designs of Dugald Drummond. Built in 1907, No. 419 was withdrawn from service in 1962 and purchased by the Scottish Railway Preservation Society. Its beautiful dark-blue livery and elaborate tank-side crests drew many admiring glances during the cavalcade.

When in 1923 the railway companies grouped into four great railways the LNER inherited many ancient and varied classes of locomotive, most of which were incapable of performing the duties the LNER envisaged. Several new classes were designed and built to counter these shortcomings, one of which was the D49 class, introduced in 1927. Before then Mr Gresley had confined the use of three cylinders to larger locomotives like the *Flying Scotsman*, but with the introduction of the D49 class, the three-cylinder design became standard for passenger locomotives on the LNER. Seventy-six locomotives were built to this design and the one prominent in this picture at Shildon shed shunting LNER class V2, 2–6–2, No. 4771 *Green Arrow* is LNER class D49 4–4–0, No. 246 *Morayshire*, number eight in the cavalcade.

GWR class 'Manor', 4–6–0, No. 7808 *Cookham Manor* being coaled at the coalyard of Dunn Bros of Shildon in readiness for the anniversary cavalcade. It was number ten in the procession. The 'Manor' class, lightweight, two-cylinder passenger locomotives mark the final stage of the Great Western Railway standardization policy of 4–6–0 steam locomotives for passenger services. During the 1960s they were mostly based in the Welsh holiday areas, Devon and Cornwall. They hauled important trains, and those allocated to the Aberystwyth depot for the 'Cambrian Coast Express' duties became famed for their polished copper and brass and spotless paintwork.

This GWR class 'Modified Hall', 4–6–0, No. 6960 *Ravingham Hall*, was number eleven in the cavalcade. In 1972 it was rescued from Barry and restored, mainly by volunteers, at Steamtown, Carnforth.

Built in 1943 to meet the urgent wartime needs of the Ministry of Supply, this 'Austerity' class 9F locomotive, 2–10–0, No. 600 *Gordon* was named after General 'Chinese' Gordon of Khartoum. This class of locomotive, along with the more numerous 2–8–0 variant, totalled over 900 examples, most of which were sent overseas towards the end of the Second World War to assist in restoring rail traffic in many countries. No. 600 remained in the UK where it was used by the British Army at the Longmoor Military Railway in Hampshire for instructional purposes. Material shortages and wartime production difficulties compelled the designer to produce a locomotive that was flexible and powerful, yet easy to build and maintain. Thus the outline of the 600, which carries no unnecessary embellishments, is stark and businesslike when compared to the other locomotives in the cavalcade. Originally wearing liveries of khaki and green, it is seen here, number fifteen in the cavalcade, in its final wartime blue livery towing LTE No. 12, *Sarah Siddons*.

LNER class A4, 4–6–2, No. 4498, *Sir Nigel Gresley*, seen here without its side valances and not fully streamlined, was built in 1937. It was the 100th Pacific locomotive to be built to Mr Gresley's design. In order to achieve maximum efficiency at high speed, the front of the locomotive was wedge-shaped with side valances, which were later removed and the tender given smooth lines to complete the effect. The tender on *Sir Nigel Gresley* is similar to that on the *Flying Scotsman* and has a corridor and a water scoop. On non-stop runs between London and Edinburgh the locomotive crews were changed en route using the corridor from their compartment in the train's leading coach some 8 miles north of York. The A4s are developed from the A3 class and thirty-five of them were built for fast non-stop runs between London and northern cities on the LNER system. In 1957, while hauling a private excursion, *Sir Nigel Gresley* attained a speed of 113mph, which has never been equalled by a steam locomotive. In 1967, when in private ownership, it hauled a special 385 ton train over Shap in Westmorland in a faster time than had previously been recorded. When *Sir Nigel Gresley* was built Garter Blue was LNER livery, the colour used on that locomotive. Other class A4 locomotives had liveries of either silver or buried-green, according to the type of train they were intended to haul. *Sir Nigel Gresley* was number sixteen in the cavalcade.

During a working life of nearly forty years LNER class A3, 4–6–2, No. 4472 *Flying Scotsman* travelled more than 2 million miles in traffic. It was built in 1923, the third of a new class of A1 Pacifics. Along with fifty-one similar locomotives, it provided the recently formed LNER with first-class express power on its main line. All the A1 locomotives were rebuilt to class A3 with high-pressure boilers and other improvements, and eventually this class totalled seventy-eight. Each locomotive carried a name, most from famous racehorses. *Flying Scotsman* became No. 4472 on its conversion to A3. During the 1930s, in defiance of prevailing economic conditions and as a reaction to the slump, races between the big four railway companies were established. They began with the GWR, which ran what disgusted rivals called a 'stunt train'. Sir Nigel Gresley, a key figure in these races, introduced more efficient 'buck-eye' couplings and articulated carriages with a single bogie supporting two coaches. But, being something of a self-publicist, he was concerned not only with speed but also in the capacity of locomotives to run non-stop between London and Scotland. With this in mind, he introduced the 'corridor' tender which enabled crews to change midway along the 392 miles between London and Edinburgh. The *Flying Scotsman* had such a tender, which was something of a gimmick because in reality the time saved on the journey was only 4½ minutes. The tender had 9 tons of coal and 5,400 gallons of water. It was also possible for water to be picked up while the train was in motion by lowering a scoop from beneath the tender into water troughs. The 'Flying Scotsman' started to run non-stop between London and Edinburgh in 1928 and it really was a very special train with luxurious carriages, ladies' hairdresser, cinema and cocktail bar. The *Flying Scotsman* is considered by many to be the most famous of all the steam locomotives and to epitomize the glorious age of steam. In the cavalcade it was number seventeen.

GNR class U, 4-4-2, No. 990 *Henry Oakley* was designed by the GNR's Chief Engineer Ivatt to fill a requirement for a more powerful engine than the 'Stirling Singles' to haul the heavy dining- and sleeping-car trains being introduced towards the end of the nineteenth century on the East Coast main line. Twenty-one of these Atlantics were built, of which *Henry Oakley* was the first; it was named after the GNR's General Manager of the day. The Atlantics were superheated to improve their steam capabilities and the addition of an extended smokebox to accommodate the superheater improved their outward appearance. *Henry Oakley* was once the pride of the British railway system and in about 1900 hauled the 'Flying Scotsman'. It was withdrawn from service in 1937, restored and painted in its original livery. *Henry Oakley* took part in the 1925 S&DR centenary, the 1953 centenary of Doncaster works, where it was built, and was number eighteen in the S&DR's 150th anniversary cavalcade.

Although the building plate on *Hardwicke* reads 'Crewe 1873', this LNWR 'President' class locomotive, 2-4-0, No. 790 was built in 1892. During the famous railway races from London to Aberdeen in 1895 *Hardwicke* proved its worth on the section allocated to it from Crewe to Carlisle where it made twenty-two racing trips totalling 3,152 miles. On 22 August of that year it covered the distance of 141 miles in 126 minutes; and that includes a climb of 915 ft over Shap at 62.4mph pulling almost three times its own weight. It was withdrawn from service in 1932. In the cavalcade it was number nineteen.

Hardwicke and Midland Compound, 4–4–0, No. 1000 leaving York on temporary loan from the National Railway Museum to Carnforth, April 1976. Compound No. 1000 was the first of 240 locomotives of this Compound design, the final series being built in 1932, well into the LMS days. Compounds worked the whole of the Midland system and in the following LMS days were used successfully in Scotland. No. 1000 was withdrawn from service in 1951. It was number twenty in the cavalcade.

This is a Pug, and fifty-seven of these 0–4–0 saddle tanks, small shunting locomotives were built for use in docks and sharply curved factory sidings by the Lancashire & Yorkshire Railway between 1891 and 1910. No. 51218 was built in 1901; it was number twenty-four in the cavalcade.

Southern Railways' 'Merchant Navy' class of locomotive was designed by the head of locomotive design at Southern Railway, O.V.S. Bulleid, one-time pupil at Doncaster works who became personal assistant to Mr Gresley. The 'Merchant Navy' class regularly hauled famous trains like 'Golden Arrow', 'Night Ferry', 'Bournemouth Belle' and the 'Atlantic Coast Express'. Bulleid liked to try new ideas and 'Merchant Navy' locomotives were fitted with many novel features, some of which were very expensive to maintain. So the class as a whole was rebuilt between 1956 and 1959. The locomotives, which were named after shipping lines, were all withdrawn by 1967. SR/BR 'Merchant Navy' class, 4-6-2, No. 35028 *Clan Line* was built in 1948 and later rebuilt. It was number twenty-seven in the carnival.

Built at Swindon Works in 1960, BR class 9, 2–10–0, No. 92220 *Evening Star* was the last steam locomotive in the cavalcade, number thirty-one, and the last steam locomotive built for British Railways. Robert Stephenson built the original *Evening Star* in 1839, but, whereas the original had only two driving wheels, the last one had ten. *Evening Star* was impressive and functional with more wheels than most and lots of power. It worked all over the country on heavy freights and was frequently seen hauling huge iron-ore trains up the steep gradients to Consett Iron Works. Although primarily a freight locomotive, it also worked passenger trains and expresses, reaching a maximum speed of 90mph. *Evening Star*, the last of Britain's steam locomotives, brought the age of railway steam to its end on a high.

During the run up to the 150th S&DR celebrations the organizers received this letter of support from Elizabeth, the Queen Mother, a typically lovely and thoughtful gesture.

There was no lack of inventiveness when it came to the design of plates to commemorate the S&DR's 150th anniversary, as these plates illustrate. The plates were on sale at the North Road Railway Museum.

This photograph of the *North Briton* at speed in 1952 captures the age of railway steam at its magnificent best. It evokes all the romance and the thrill of thundering through the countryside hauled by a powerful steam locomotive. But changes were afoot. In January 1955 the Chairman of the Railway Executive Sir Brian Robertson published a £1,200 million Modernisation Plan which would take fifteen years to complete and which, he believed, would totally revolutionize the whole railway system and which laid the foundation stones for Inter-City in the 1960s. He had the vision, the managerial skill and intellect to provide Britain with an efficient rail system attuned to the country's social and economic needs. It was in the Beeching Report of 1963 that the term Inter-city was first used to loosely describe the whole long-distance rail network. Beeching's philosophy was simplicity itself. 'I see the railways as a national asset owned by the Nation and therefore to be used in the best interests of the Nation as a whole. My job and that of the British Railways Board is to run the railways in the best interests of the whole community.' He was firm, determined, courteous and wily. 'If you have a sticky problem,' he once told a colleague, 'work out an answer, create chaos and then offer up the solution.' He also had a sense of humour. Once on seeing some graffiti in a station lavatory which said 'Beeching is a prat', he added a firm, 'no I'm not'. When he arrived at BR he found a complete absence of statistical analysis and financial awareness, but saw that half of BR's 7,000 stations processed a mere 2 per cent of its total traffic. At a time when railways faced insuperable obstacles in their struggle against the lorry and with car ownership rapidly increasing, it was ridiculous to suppose that all 3,500 of these could be worth preserving. Out came Beeching's infamous axe. It was against this background that, on 21 May 1967, the S&DR stopped being a through route from Stockton to Darlington. The stretch of line between the S&D crossing at the Darlington end and Paton and Baldwins Mill was closed and the S&D crossing signal-box removed.

During the 1960s people remained loyal to the railways. Throughout Britain, on both local and main lines, passenger trains were becoming steadily busier, passengers being carried on a railway system that in pre-Beeching days was much larger. During the summer-holiday periods trains carried record numbers of passengers to seaside resorts like Scarborough, helped by the pulling power of publicity posters like this one.

British Railways publicity people were quick to point out the advantages of going by train to quaint fishing villages along the Yorkshire coast – and it worked. Despite Beeching's axe, this really was the age of the train. It had to be – British Railways publicity said so.

Durham Light Infantry cadets alongside the locomotive named after their famous regiment, 19 June 1961. They are commemorating the bicentenary of the DLI which was raised in 1758.

The name is the same, but all else is updated. This is a 'Deltic', D9017, which on 29 October 1963 was named *Durham Light Infantry*. As work progressed on West Coast electrification, BR bought high-powered diesel locomotives for the East Coast route's passenger services between Kings Cross, Leeds, Darlington, Newcastle and Scotland. Facing competition from private cars and expanding domestic air services, the forward-looking East Coast management decided to wait no longer for electrification. Fortunately, the English Electric Company had shown some real foresight in designing and building a new high-powered diesel prototype locomotive at their own expense. It was called the 'Deltic' and was way ahead of its time.

D5094 was the first main-line diesel-electric built at the North Road Works, Darlington, and it is seen here setting out on a trial run on 21 January 1960. This type of locomotive was deemed to be non-standard by 1977, and withdrawals started during the decline of railways. During 1977 another section of the S&DR closed, from Paton and Baldwin's Mill to Fighting Cocks Crossing, and the line was lifted in 1978.

BR's Area Manager Peter Fearnhead (left) and the Mayor of Darlington, Councillor Jim Skinner with Inter-City 125 *Darlington* – what else? – at Darlington's Bank Top station, May 1984. At the ceremony the Mayor receives a model of the 125 *Darlington*. Between 1982 and 1986 Inter-City lost its hyphen, becoming simply Intercity. This began the process of creating a new and distinctive image for Intercity, now an independent business as well as a brand name.

On Friday 27 September 1985, exactly 160 years since the opening of the S&DR and exactly fifty years since the record-breaking run of the *Silver Jubilee*, HST power car No. 43038 passes the National Railway Museum at York where class A4, 4-6-2, No. 4468 *Mallard*, in steam but without its streamline casing, is in the company of GNR No. 1.

A Brush/BR-built Type 4, class 47 at Newton Aycliffe station, 9 November, 1984. This is one of the largest fleet of diesel locomotives associated with Intercity, numbering over 500 built between 1963 and 1967 for main-line passenger and freight work; it operated to virtually all parts of the BR network and was associated with the development of many Intercity routes. The class 47 did not operate along that section of the S&DR between Fighting Cocks and Oak Tree Junction after 1988 because that was the year the section closed. The rail welding depot at Dinsdale closed at the same time. The section from Oak Tree Junction to Eaglescliffe, originally known as Preston Junction, is still open on the original track. The S&DR continued from the then Preston Junction via Preston Park to Stockton Docks. In 1849 Yarm viaduct was built and in 1852 the Leeds North Railway from Leeds to Stockton via Yarm was opened and the original S&DR link from Eaglescliffe station to Bowesfield Junction became redundant and was closed. Dock closed in 1964 and after 142 years of operating, the line from Eaglescliffe to Stockton Dock closed in 1967.

CHAPTER ELEVEN

The S&DR Remembered: 175 Years On

Throughout the 175-year history of the S&DR steam has been its main driving force, and the locomotives depicted in this chapter are proud representatives of that memorable age which saw the railways grow into a worldwide network. The GNER Intercity 225 high-speed electric train, seen here on 30 June 1999, on the East Coast route epitomizes today's railway system at its best – it is the car's worst advertisement. In April 1994 Britain's railway system was denationalized. This happened at a time when air travel had become almost as commonplace as catching a bus and with car ownership at an all time high. Yet, far from being a nineteenth-century anachronism, the railway system was seen as having the potential to solve many of the transport problems that the internal combustion engine had created. Moreover, it could do so efficiently and often more cheaply. The denationalized railway system was on the threshold of dramatic progress in speed and the bulk movement of freight, with advanced technology being exploited in every area of railway operations. Electricity traction was the key. It provided the best kind of service, being clean, fast and reliable with substantial cost savings in maintenance and fuel consumption compared with diesel traction. The only disadvantages were substantial capital outlay and disturbance to existing services during the change-over period.

The future is built on the past, and from 27–30 September 2000 the opening of the S&DR 175 years ago will be celebrated. For without the S&DR, and other railways emanating from it, the mass movement of people, raw materials and finished products would never have happened when it did and the UK would never have become the workshop of the world.

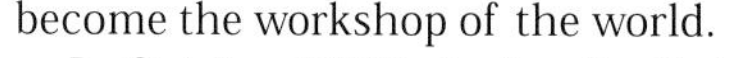

In October 1829, during the Rainhill Trials to decide how trains on the Liverpool & Manchester would be powered, Robert Stephenson's *Rocket* attained a steady 29mph on its later runs, proving that his design was far more reliable than the competing locomotives. By the end of 1830 the *Rocket* had been replaced by the *Northumbrian*, another of Robert Stephenson's designs and the first engine to be built with an integral firebox. It was the same as that fitted to every orthodox locomotive ever since. Within a few years the immortal *Rocket* had been relegated to the sidings. Here it is seen in full steam at the National Railway Museum, York.

A replica of the famous *Sanspareil* locomotive letting off steam on 30 August 1937. An advertisement in the *Liverpool Mercury* of 1 May 1829 invited contestants to enter the Rainhill Trials. One of the entries considered suitable was *Sanspareil* from Timothy Hackworth's New Shildon Works. *Sanspareil's* original wheels had wooden spokes, but the second set was made entirely of iron. It was painted green, yellow and black with a white chimney. It was disqualified at the trials because it was too heavy and had no springs.

LNER class V2, 2–6–2, No. 4771 *Green Arrow* is one of five locomotives built in 1936 as forerunners of a new class designed to meet the ever-increasing demands of the day for fast and reliable mixed-traffic locomotion. No. 4771 regularly hauled the 3.55 p.m. 'Scottish Goods' north from London. It worked remarkably well for so heavy a train. Later it met equal success in the hilly regions of Scotland. So successfully did the V2 operate that further numbers were built and at the start of the Second World War almost 100 of these locomotives were in service. *Green Arrow* is now based at the National Railway Museum, York.

Mallard, the greatest steam locomotive in the world, is seen here hauling the eight-coach 'Aberdeen Flyer' carrying 300 passengers on its historic run between Kings Cross and Edinburgh, a distance of 392 miles. It was the longest non-stop journey ever by an excursion train in this country.

LNER Pacific 4–6–2, No. 60009, *Union of South Africa* was the last A4 to run non-stop from Kings Cross to Edinburgh, 26 October 1964. On the outward trip it was 53 minutes late arriving at Newcastle. On the return journey it was 2 minutes late leaving Newcastle but covered 80 miles in 80 minutes to reach York 3 minutes early. The round trip was called 'Jubilee Requiem' because it was the last chance to ride behind an A4. When the *Union of South Africa* left Kings Cross for the engine shed the driver blew a long blast of the whistle.

LNER 532/BR60532, class A2, 4–6–2, *Blue Peter* hauls a special excursion train, the 'Cumbrian Mountain Express', out of Garsdale station, March 1992. It is the only surviving example of the designs of Arthur H. Peppercorn, the last Chief Mechanical Engineer of the LNER before nationalization in 1948. Although constructed by the LNER, *Blue Peter* No. 532 was not delivered until 25 March 1948 and appeared as No. 60532 with 'British Railways' displayed on its tender. At first it worked main-line trains from its base at York. Then it was transferred to Scotland where it remained until its withdrawal from service on 31 December 1966. The locomotive's name is derived from the international code flag 'P' used by vessels about to leave port. It was also the name of the 1939 Derby and 2000 Guineas winner owned by Lord Rosebery.

LMS 'Princess Royal' class, 4-6-2, No. 6201 *Princess Elizabeth* was born in 1930 when prestige trains of the four great railway companies were becoming faster and heavier, and seen here in the 1990s, still operational. It was a time when speed records were made and broken in rapid succession and *Princess Elizabeth* is a world record breaker. In 1936 she hauled a test train from London to Glasgow in 5 hours 52 minutes, returning in 5 hours 44 minutes, covering a distance of 800 miles at an average speed of over 70mph. Unlike later Pacifics the 'Princess Royal' class looked rugged, powerful and fast. They had to be. Their home ground, the West Coast main line, had severe gradients like Beattock and Shap as well as fast stretches.

LMS class 5 MT, 4-6-0, No. 4767 *George Stephenson* at Wylam for the bicentenary of George Stephenson's birth, June 1981. This locomotive has an excellent pedigree and is often described as one of the most successful engines built by the LMS. It is one of 842 Stanier-designed locomotives and was first introduced in 1934 for work on either freight or express passenger duties, where it was unsurpassed. *George Stephenson* was fitted with Stephenson's valve gear, a design originally introduced by George Stephenson more than a hundred years earlier. It was the last main-line locomotive in England to be fitted with an outside Stephenson's valve gear. Over the years *George Stephenson* gained a reputation for being stronger in acceleration on or climbing against the gradient than its sister engines. However, because the age of steam on British Rail was coming to an end, No. 4767 was withdrawn from service in 1967. It was then privately purchased as No. 44767 and during 1975 was completely overhauled and restored to its original livery as No. 4767 by its owner, Ian Storey.

Shortly after the formation of the LNER the *Flying Scotsman*, a class 3, 4–6–2, locomotive, No. 4472, was built in 1923. It was a very special train, the height of luxury during the interwar years.

Cuneo's superb painting of the 'Flying Scotsman' going over the Forth Bridge captures all the power and majesty of this fantastic train.

This Ashington Colliery locomotive No. 6, 0–6–0, was built by Peckett and Son, Bristol, and is now housed at the Stephenson Railway Museum, North Tyneside. It is pictured here on the North Tyneside Steam Railway.

The inauguration of a new service along a branch line close to Hadrian's Wall. The train, a Pacer, is called a 'Nodding Donkey' because it bounces along the track. The Roman soldiers were present as part of a publicity event.

Pretty Fanny Kemble, a member of the most distinguished theatrical family in London, attended the Rainhill Trials in 1829. She climbed on to the footplate of the *Rocket* with George Stephenson, and was beside herself with admiration for the man from Newcastle who had 'certainly turned my head'. She was not alone. Both in Britain and abroad George Stephenson had turned many heads with his technical capacities and his flair for public relations, reinforced by his son's more formal engineering designs. Within a few years of Rainhill, the *Rocket* had been relegated to the sidings, but it had proved that a mobile steam locomotive could replace the horses and stationary engines that everyone had assumed were essential to conquer even the smallest gradients. Two years after Rainhill, in 1831, large numbers of people were travelling in locomotive-drawn carriages, as this drawing illustrates. The unimaginable had happened.

This Intercity photograph of the first-class interior of an Intercity 225 electric train showing the meal service would have had Fanny Kemble and George Stephenson drooling. In 1879 the first restaurant car ran on a British railway. For 121 years the quality of railway food has been a matter of lively public debate and often the butt of music-hall jokes. Not any more: today the food and drink served on Intercity are arguably the best and most cost effective anywhere in Europe.

The S&DR helped to create a revolution that spread throughout the world, but now part of the track that runs along the first passenger route in the world has been officially closed to rail traffic. On 24 April 1969 workmen removed the gates at the level crossing in Bridge Street, Stockton, close to the line's first ticket office, an historic and dilapidated building seen on the left in the background here. Then they put up a fence on both sides of the road, effectively sealing off rail access to the old Stockton Quay, which was one of the mainstays of trade for Stockton during the nineteenth century. The quay was closed in 1967, since when the S&DR sidings have been idle. The signal-cabin near the crossing was demolished in 1968 and the corrugated-iron sheds that once housed the little shunting engines have all gone.

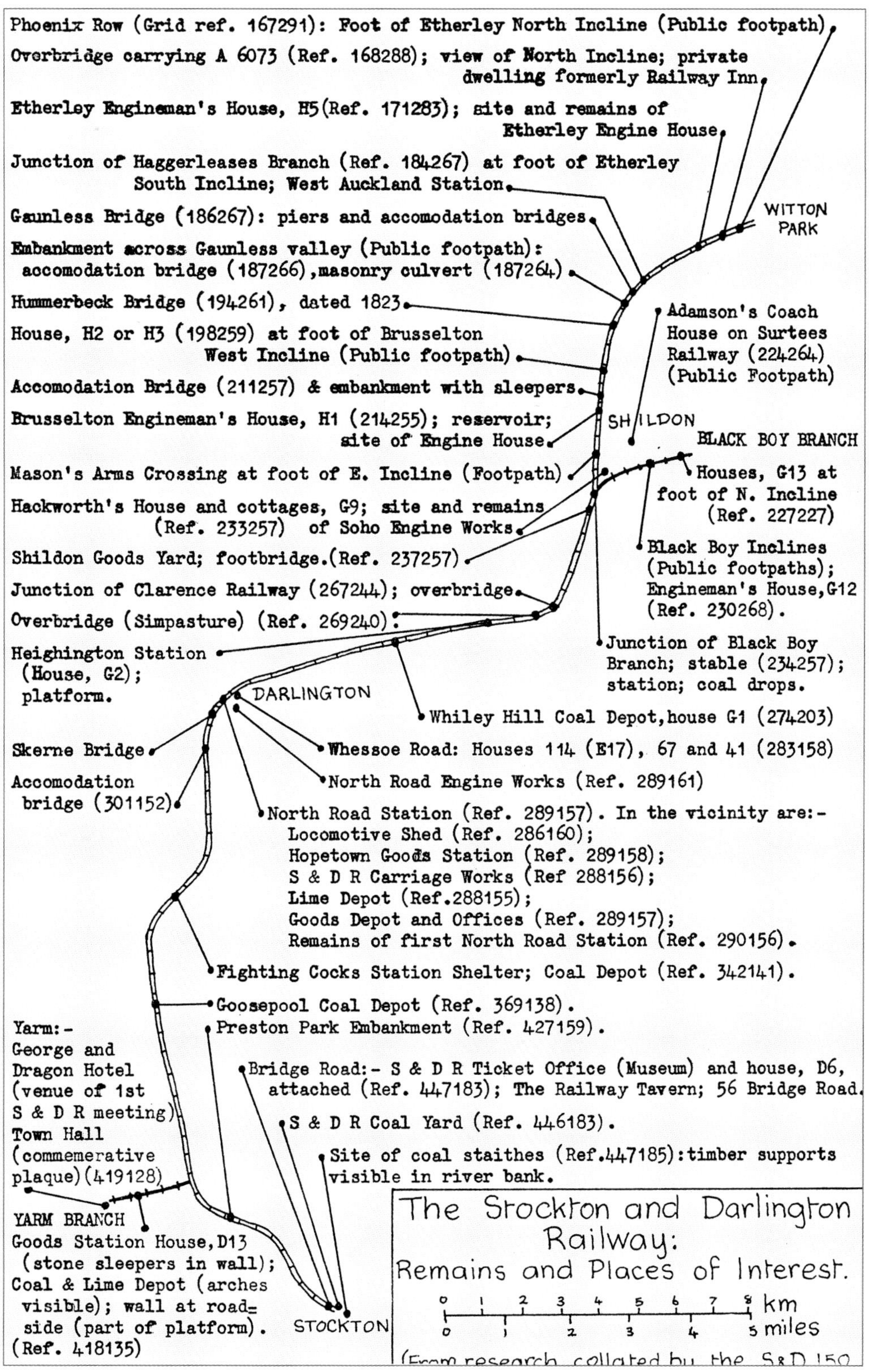

The S&DR is not dead, however, and a truncated section between Shildon and Darlington remains. The rest has been confined to history, yet the line's illustrious legacy lives on. This outline of the S&DR details what still exists of the line and places of interest.

The shape of things to come: electrification. Here a 225 Intercity hauls a full set of Mark IV coaches during acceptance trials on 6 October 1994.

When, in 1995, this Intercity 225 broke the UK speed record for trains, it opened up a new railway era, one that is already transforming the system that today leads in railway engineering and development. Much of the credit for it must go to the visionaries who conceived the S&DR, which, in turn, did much to open up a new industrial age powered by steam. Now 175 years on electrification is pointing the way to a new and even brighter dawn, and all the signals are at 'Go'.